THE STORY OF
SOUTHAMPTON

THE STORY OF
SOUTHAMPTON

PETER NEAL

The
History
Press

First published 2014

The History Press
The Mill, Brimscombe Port
Stroud, Gloucestershire, GL5 2QG
www.thehistorypress.co.uk

British Library Cataloguing in Publication Data.
A catalogue record for this book is available from the British Library.

ISBN 978 1 86077 674 8

Typesetting and origination by The History Press
Printed in Great Britain

CONTENTS

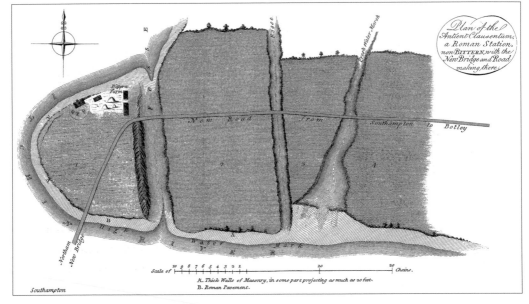

Plan of the Clausentum. (Courtesy of Southampton Record Office)

ACKNOWLEDGEMENTS

As is customary, I must pay tribute to the many people who have so graciously and selflessly assisted me in the writing of this book, without whom I would not have been able to achieve all that I have. First and foremost, my gratitude goes to the staff at the Local Studies section of Southampton City Library, who have so helpfully and efficiently dealt with my queries. I am particularly thankful to Vicky Green and Penny Rudkin, while Dave Hollingworth played a crucial role in organising the use of many of the photographic images of Southampton that have been reproduced in the book. Additional help with the photographs was provided by David Rymill at Hampshire Record Office and Lindsay Mulholland at Associated British Ports. I must also thank my family and friends for their interest and encouragement, with a special mention to my mum, whose faith in me has been unwavering.

West Gate, Southampton. (Library of Congress, LC-DIG-ppmsc-08846)

INTRODUCTION

As with all towns and cities, Southampton has seen a great many changes in the 2,000 years of history covered in this book – from humble beginnings as a small Roman settlement to the busy, sprawling metropolis of modern times. Its genesis lay in its location as a seaport with access to both the southern half of England and routes to Europe and beyond – a pivotal point through which both people and trade have passed for two millennia. The shelter afforded by the Isle of Wight and the associated double tide that its position benefits from have meant that this traffic has come through Southampton for much of this period.

Of course, fate and fortune have fluctuated over the years and, like any other town, Southampton has known good times and bad in this period. From the depths of destitution following a French raid in 1338 to the ocean-going boom of the mid-twentieth century, when the greatest and largest ships of the day steamed in and out of the port. Promotional posters once declared Southampton the 'Gateway to the World' and, although the glamour and grace of the *Queen Mary* and *Queen Elizabeth* have gone forever, Southampton is still primarily a portal to distant lands across the seas – whether it is for holidaymakers, or for the thousands of consumer goods that leave and enter the port every day.

With 2014 marking the fifty-year anniversary of Southampton being granted city status, it is appropriate that this work relates its entire story and allows its own citizens and others alike to appreciate the rich and varied events that have created the Southampton we know today.

Peter Neal, 2014

one

BEGINNINGS

T he Roman invasion of Britain in AD 43 was met with little resistance initially, but was followed by two large battles, the first of which was at Rochester in Kent and the second at the point where the Romans came to cross the Thames. Here they waited until joined by their emperor, Claudius, who led his men to the triumphal climax of the first stage of the invasion – the conquest of the British stronghold Camulodunum (today's Colchester). The town was the capital of the Catuvellauni region and the Romans made it their first capital of Britain.

Once Camulodunum had been taken, legions were dispatched to extend the Roman invasion into other areas of the country. One of these, II Legion, was led by Vespasian, who in AD 69 would become head of the entire Roman Empire. Vespasian took his men in a south-westerly direction, and by AD 47, the conquest had reached as far as Somerset and Devon. For the time being at least, this was the extent of the Roman conquest in this area: Claudius's commander-in-chief Aulus Plautius returned to Rome in triumph with his part in the operation complete. It is thus fair to say that the Romans had a presence in Hampshire and the Isle of Wight within a few years of the initial invasion. The theory has been expressed that a temporary naval and supply base at Clausentum may have existed before AD 50 to service the Romans' ongoing western progress, but greater certainty can be attached to the existence of a port in the location in about AD 70.

By this time, the Romans had established a sizeable town at Venta Belgarum (Winchester), the site of a previous tribal capital. The town created a demand for items such as wine and oil that the new residents wished to enjoy in their new homes as they had on the Continent. Thus, a port was needed, and trade routes to Gaul were soon in place, with exports such as wool, corn and even slaves crossing the Channel in return. Clausentum was located on the eastern bank of the River Itchen, around 3 miles inland from what is now known as

Southampton Water. It was sited on a peninsula created by a curve in the river and was divided into islands by two fosses (large ditches) running from north to south. The western island was approximately semi-circular in shape, with its curved edge following that of the river, while the second island was almost rectangular. This rectangular island was sparsely occupied by a few wooden-framed buildings; however, it was the semi-circular island that the Romans chose for most of their habitation. It was reached by a road that led away from the main gate, across the second island, and joined a road linking Winchester and Portchester. Originally, the island is likely to have been edged by a fence punctuated by towers and accessed by a main gate that overlooked the fosse. When it was first dug, the inner fosse was around 60ft wide and was made yet wider over the following decades, up to about 100ft. At particularly high tides, the fosse was partially filled with water, even as late as the nineteenth century.

There was at least one road within the fenced area of Clausentum, traces of which were uncovered when graves were dug in Bitterne cemetery. It was formed with a lower layer of limestone and topped with a covering of gravel, and possibly terminated at the riverside, since evidence has been found on the riverbank of a wooden quayside built to accommodate Roman shipping. An important discovery in 1918 added weight to this theory, when two lead pigs were discovered during the construction of foundations at a riverside site. The lead pigs were found at a depth of around 2½ft, weighed almost 180lb and were about 2ft in length. They were engraved with text dating them to the Vespasian period and were thought to have originated from the Mendip lead mines. It is possible that the lead had initially been transported to the Continent to be cast into shape, and the pigs were making their return journey when they were somehow deposited in the Itchen. The discovery led to a further hypothesis that Clausentum and Venta Belgarum were linked by road at an early stage following the Roman invasion; the fact that stone from the Isle of Wight was used in buildings in Venta Belgarum makes the road connection even more likely.

Bembridge limestone from the Isle of Wight was used at Clausentum as well as Venta Belgarum, for example in a private bathing house uncovered during excavations in 1951. This structure was adjacent to another larger building near the northern town perimeter in the area later occupied by Bitterne Manor House. During the first century of the Roman occupation of Britain, great quantities of marble were extracted from the Purbeck quarries in Dorset. Since stone from them was used as far afield as Chichester, Cirencester and Colchester, it seems highly likely to have featured in at least some of the buildings of Clausentum as well. The Purbeck area was also home to many pottery kilns, some dating from the first century AD, and a network of Roman roads allowed the pottery to be distributed throughout the region. In later years, the kilns in the New Forest increased their production, with the pieces making the shorter journey to Clausentum.

The town's life as a port linking central England and Gaul lasted around two centuries, and towards the end of this period, it was mentioned in a Roman text for the only time: the Antonine Itinerary recorded routes used by the Romans and the distances between towns. At about the same time wooden houses first built in the settlement were gradually replaced with stone structures. The third century brought with it the period known as the 'occupation gap', during which there is little evidence of significant activity in Clausentum. Suggestions have been put forward that the town was affected, to one degree or another, by a fire and subsequently fell into disrepair; but this is merely one theory. Therefore, the 'occupation gap' may be more accurately thought of as a gap in evidence and knowledge, rather than a time in which Clausentum was necessarily deserted.

As the third century neared its close, changes in Roman thinking meant that the friendly welcome previously afforded to visitors from overseas was replaced with a more cautious policy. Many of the ports along the South Coast were more heavily fortified and took on defensive roles. It was at this time that Carausius, having previously been a naval captain stationed in the North Sea and English Channel, evidently suffered from delusions of grandeur. In 286, he declared himself emperor of Britain and northern Gaul, seemingly with a mind to create his own breakaway empire using Britannia as its base. Carausius relocated his fleet from Boulogne to the Solent, and it is thought that he envisaged Clausentum as a main defensive stronghold in the area, in conjunction with the impressive fortifications at Portchester. For many years, speculation has abounded that Carausius founded a mint at Clausentum, but no firm evidence has been uncovered to settle the debate. In 293, Carausius was murdered by his treasurer Allectus, who in turn was overthrown three years later when the patience of the Roman Empire based in mainland Europe was finally exhausted. Julius Asclepiodotus and his forces set sail from Boulogne and under cover of fog landed in Hampshire to quash the separatist empire of Britannia.

Rule from Italy resumed, but in 367 Roman Britain found itself under attack again, with Saxons venturing across the North Sea and Picts making southerly incursions from central Scotland and beyond. Towns were ransacked, livestock stolen and men held captive by the invaders. The result in Clausentum was that in about 370 the town was further reinforced by a strong, stone wall that was built around its perimeter. Count Theodosius had become the civil governor of Britain in 368 and undertook a scheme to renovate much of the British defences, most probably in response to these raids. Archaeologists excavating in the early 1950s also agreed that during this period (and again in about 390) there was renewed building activity inside the walled town. The wall itself was approximately 9ft thick and gained a large amount of its rigidity from a bonding course of large, flat bricks running through it. It was built without foundations, however, and therefore required further strengthening in the form of a bank of earth packed against it on the inward side.

Sir Henry Englefield toured Southampton at the start of the nineteenth century and recorded that some Roman remains were still visible even at this late stage. He speculated that there might have been another inner wall of about 2ft in thickness, providing extra support to the earthen bank, although he found no conclusive proof. Englefield also wrote that traces of at least two Roman towers were uncovered, set into the town wall. These towers were approximately 18ft in diameter and there was evidence of a further semi-circular tower or buttress of slightly greater dimensions. But the extra fortifications were not to stand the test of time. In about 411, the Romans departed British shores, since Rome was under attack from the Goths, and the emperor, Honorius, relocated his centre of operations to Constantinople. From this more easterly base, Britain was more distant and thus proportionately also less important – so the Roman troops withdrew. In doing so they created what has been described as 'one of the genuinely fateful moments in British history'.

With his country at the mercy of invaders once more, legend has it that British leader, Vortigern, decided to make a pact with the Saxons: in exchange for land on the Isle of Thanet they would repel the renewed advances of the Picts. When it became apparent that Vortigern saw this agreement as a one-off deal rather than an ongoing arrangement, the Saxons were considerably aggrieved and revolted in spectacular fashion, with southern and eastern England suffering most in the turmoil. Some towns were reduced significantly in size while others were completely deserted. Houses, roads and public buildings fell into disrepair. It is probable that the Saxons laid waste to Clausentum at this time, and towards the end of the fifth century, Cerdic and his son, Cynric, landed at a location in the vicinity. They established the kingdom of Wessex in 519, seeing Winchester as an important base because of its strategic positioning in the network of Roman roads. Cerdic ruled for fifteen years until he died, and was succeeded by his son, and for many years afterwards, kings of Wessex claimed him as one of their ancestors.

In 530, the Saxons embarked on the conquest of the Isle of Wight in collaboration with the Jutes, probably departing from a point near Clausentum. Most Romano-British people must have wanted reassurance that their leaders would offer them the best possible protection, while the leaders no doubt required a subservient and hard-working population. Eventually these two sets of demands intertwined and parity was restored.

For many years, the ruins of Clausentum were left to the remaining native Britons in the area and the elements. Meanwhile, the next centre of population took root on the peninsula created by the convergence of the rivers Itchen and Test. The land had been used by the Romans at least to a small extent, as evidenced by sparse archaeological finds among the plentiful Saxon material. But in the Roman era there were few inhabitants here, and they were most likely to have been engaged in farming and fishing. It was here that Birinus first landed in England in 634, embarking on his campaign to reintroduce Christianity in the country. It is said that during his visit the first incarnation of St Mary's church was established.

In the closing years of the seventh century, trade routes between Britain and north-western Europe began to flourish, and towns such as London and Ipswich conducted business with their counterparts across the North Sea in France, Holland, Denmark and even Sweden. By this time, Wessex was ruled by Ine, who introduced a series of laws reflecting his adherence to Christianity. A stable social, economic and political climate during Ine's reign contributed to an expansion in trade, but there is no documentary evidence of the port that would become Southampton until 720, when it was mentioned in the memoirs of St Willibald. A monk born in Wessex in about 700 and raised in Bishops Waltham, Willibald went on to travel throughout Europe and the Holy Land. He referred to the town as Hamwih, although it is more generally known now as Hamwic. The first part of the name, 'ham', meant home, while the second was derived from the Latin 'vicus', meaning a town or part of a town. This suffix also formed the names of other centres of trading, such as Harwich and Norwich. Hamwic stood on the shores of a harbour naturally formed at the south-eastern corner of the peninsula by a combination of winds and currents. These factors created a shingle spit that curved northwards into the Itchen Estuary and made a small sheltered bay in which vessels could land safely.

The town was thus bounded directly to the east by the River Itchen and to the south and the north-east by marshland. The westerly limitation of the settlement was defined by a ditch that was 10ft wide, meaning that the total area enclosed was more than 100 acres. A substantial network of roads was built in the town, roughly on a grid pattern. The main street, approximately on the route of today's St Mary's Road, was 50ft wide, and other narrower streets joined it on either side. All the roads were finished with a top layer of gravel and were well maintained, being resurfaced when needed. This degree of planning and upkeep perhaps implies that Hamwic was governed by some kind of authority or council.

The houses in the settlement were mostly timber framed with thatched roofs, although it is possible that a few remnants of Clausentum were appropriated and recycled. Archaeology shows that the houses were rectangular, one-storey buildings up to 40ft long and 16ft wide. They were well weatherproofed and would have lasted around thirty years before needing to be rebuilt. Since land in Hamwic was at a premium, houses were often rebuilt several times on the same plot. Occasionally, houses were divided into two rooms, possibly with one serving as a living area and the other for sleeping. Some directly fronted the gravelled streets, while others were reached by alleyways. Backyards contained rubbish pits, many hundreds of which have been excavated in recent years. The number and depth of these pits suggests that Hamwic was densely populated, and that the back streets and alleyways were quite congested. In some cases, the back-yards also included wells, which supplied nearby houses with fresh water. They were kept an appropriate distance from the rubbish pits to avoid contamination, and were braced with planks and wattle for rigidity. Wells were several yards deep and water was extracted by the simple method of a bucket on a rope.

The port at Hamwic served Winchester and the surrounding areas in much the same way as Clausentum had previously, trading with northern and central Europe. Pottery and glass from these areas have been found; fragments of containers for wine and other luxury items. Further evidence of this trade has been uncovered in the form of many Saxon coins, mostly sceattas, which were widely used in eighth-century Europe. A mint was established in the town, but seemingly the coins it produced were only used in Hamwic itself, as very few of them have been found further afield. Even so, the localised trade was strong: it is thought that over 2 million sceattas were made at the mint. The majority of the coins were produced in the mid-eighth century, suggesting that this was when Hamwic's economy was at its peak. Other coins found in the area originated in northern Europe, London and Kent.

As well as trading with other towns in Britain and overseas, Hamwic had its own small-scale industries. Many iron objects were made by the local blacksmiths, whose workshops were probably adjacent to their houses. The metalwork they produced included tools such as knives and axes, as well as more intricate items, such as locks and keys. Small objects like buckles and decorative pieces were fashioned from bronze, and there is evidence that small amounts of gold and mercury gilding were also in use.

Other craftsmen in Hamwic worked with bones and antlers, which were used to make combs, spindles and needles. These items in turn were used in the production of wool and cloth: sheep were reared in the town primarily to service the wool industry rather than for food. Once the wool was made into yarn, it was then woven on looms that could produce very fine cloth, some small sections of which have been uncovered by archaeologists. Ornate edgings were also made, designed to be attached to a larger piece of material to form a decorative border. The spinning and weaving were largely done by the women of Hamwic, who became very skilled in the manufacture of cloth.

The people of Hamwic generally ate a nutritious diet, with fruits, vegetables and herbs grown in the town, and fish and shellfish available from the rivers and estuary. Only small amounts of poultry and cattle meat were consumed, while grain was brought to the town from elsewhere rather than grown nearby. The food waste uncovered by archaeologists shows an even distribution of the same kinds of remains, implying that all the residents had a similar diet, regardless of wealth or social standing. The average lifespan of the townspeople was consistent with other Saxon settlements – around thirty-five for women and slightly more for men. As may be expected, deaths in infancy were far from rare, with around a quarter of the children not reaching their tenth birthday.

Christianity, which flourished under the rule of Ine, was reflected in the construction of at least one church in Hamwic. Like the other buildings, it was timber framed with a thatched roof. Close by was a graveyard in which bodies were buried in wooden coffins, positioned on an east-to-west alignment. This type of burial is consistent with, but not exclusive to, Christian practice, so the religion of those interred cannot be stated with absolute certainty. These graves showed no evidence of the burial paraphernalia associated with earlier pagan cemeteries, but at other burial sites in the settlement weapons have been found placed alongside their former owners. Such graves, however, could conceivably be those of travellers from overseas not immersed in Christianity.

The name Hamtunscire first appeared in a charter of 755, and the *Anglo-Saxon Chronicle* and several other documents of the eighth and ninth centuries make reference to Hamtun. This name amalgamated the 'ham' from Hamwic with 'tun', meaning enclosure. For some time it was thought that Hamtun and Hamwic were the same place, but it is now considered more likely that they were adjacent but distinct areas. One historic text suggests that the perimeter of Hamtun was in fact very small – just over 200yds – and, therefore, it may have been a fortified stronghold. Hamwic has revealed no evidence of such defensive areas, so the exact location of Hamtun may never be known. Although much of its precise history is unclear, the settlement was evidently significant enough that the county was named after it, rather than the perhaps more obvious choice of Winchester.

As the eighth century became the ninth, Britain found itself under attack from new aggressors – the Vikings of Scandinavia. One of their initial landing points was in Dorset, but there was then a hiatus of some thirty years before the next major invasion. The Vikings attacked again in 835, and over the next three decades, they targeted numerous points on the British coast, predominantly in the south and east. The raids differed greatly, however, in terms of severity and duration. In some areas, such as York, the Vikings settled to create a thriving community, establishing farming and trading. Hamwic, on the other hand, was violently sacked in 842, but the perpetrators soon moved on with their ill-gotten gains, to regroup for their next skirmish elsewhere. In 860, the Danes landed at the town again, but on this occasion, the object of their mission was Winchester, which they raided. Returning to the coast, however, the 'Ealdormen of Hampshire and Berkshire', Osric and Ethelwulf, were waiting for them and duly wrought their revenge.

During the Viking attacks, it is possible that some of the people of Hamwic took refuge within the old walls of Clausentum, thus leaving their settlement at the mercy of the invaders. The Vikings also raided some of the places that Hamwic traded with, which would clearly have had a detrimental effect on its economy. Other unknown factors may have contributed to the demise of Hamwic. Whatever they might have been, by the mid- to late ninth century the place was no longer really a town. A few inhabitants remained, but the streets and buildings rapidly fell into disrepair. Some of the population is likely to have relocated to Winchester, which was expanding at the same time as Hamwic's decline. For around a century, the town saw very little significant activity.

ARCHAEOLOGICAL EXCAVATIONS AT CLAUSENTUM

The two lead pigs found in the waters of the Itchen in 1918 were by no means the only important discoveries made at the Roman site of Clausentum. Over thirty years later, in the spring of 1951, further excavations began at the behest of the Inspectorate of Ancient Monuments, part of the Ministry of Works. Work began in late March and lasted for fifteen weeks; overseeing the project was Dr Molly Aylwin Cotton. Some of the manpower and equipment was supplied by Southampton Corporation, and assistance was also given by the architect Herbert Collins, who owned part of the land on which the excavations took place. The dig centred on Bitterne Manor House and the Steuart Road vicinity, and produced many finds that served as invaluable evidence in piecing together the history of Clausentum. Success in the project was not easily achieved, however, since adverse weather conditions 'made Bitterne peninsula an unenviable spot', in the words of Dr Cotton. A little over three years later, in the summer of 1954, archaeologists led by P.W. Gathercole returned to the Clausentum site for more excavations at the junction of Bitterne Road and Steuart Road. This time the dig was on a much smaller scale, lasting only a fortnight. Good examples of pottery and coins were found, however, as well as animal remains, adding to the picture of Roman-era life in the area.

two

CANUTE, CONQUEST, CASTLE

As the settlement began to recover, it relocated to the southern part of the west of the peninsula. The precise way in which the settlement became known as Southampton is now unlikely to be proved definitively, but a number of theories have been expressed. A concept that the 'South' prefix was added to distinguish the town from Northampton is now disregarded: it may merely be that the newly occupied area was simply south of the previous Hamtun settlement. Confusingly, however, up until the sixteenth century the inhabitants still referred to the previous site of Hamwic as 'Old Hampton'. The move could at least partially be attributed to shipping conditions: the River Itchen was silting up on the peninsula's eastern shore, and furthermore the increasing size of seagoing vessels meant that the River Test to the west was more easily navigable.

A period of relative peace came to an end shortly after the accession of Ethelred in 978. Southampton was attacked in 980 and again the following year, with significant numbers of the townspeople killed or captured. In 994, the Danish king, Sweyn, chose Southampton as the location of a winter base for his troops, who arrived in almost 100 ships and forcefully entered and occupied the town. Sweyn's men had originally targeted London with limited success, and had subsequently plundered the coasts of Kent and Sussex en route to Hampshire. Unable to sustain a worthwhile defence, Ethelred agreed to pay the Vikings rather than suffer any further at their hands, and the invaders retired to Southampton while they waited for their remuneration – menaces money on a grand scale.

Despite this pact, the Danes raided Southampton and the Isle of Wight again in 1001, and received a yet greater payment in exchange for their withdrawal. Evidently realising that there was good money to be made from periodic violent forays against Ethelred's meagre defences, the Danes repeated the manoeuvre in 1006 and 1012, pocketing a larger windfall each time. By 1013, the king was a fugitive from Sweyn and barely more popular with his own people, and he escaped via Southampton and the Isle of Wight to northern France. In the aftermath of Sweyn's victory, the *Anglo-Saxon Chronicle* observed that 'all the nation regarded him as full king', but he died the following year and Ethelred returned. Sweyn's son, Canute, withdrew to Denmark, but at the time of Ethelred's death, in 1016, he was in Southampton, where he summoned the witan (a council of the wise men of Wessex) to him. The witan gave its blessing to Canute, but when Ethelred's son, Edmund, reappeared the Council's allegiance was tested; and eventually the kingdom was divided between the two contenders for the throne. However, before the end of 1016, Edmund too was dead and Canute became ruler of the entire country.

Wessex became the hub of Canute's kingdom, with Winchester retaining the significance it had enjoyed since Roman times. Both Winchester and Southampton experienced newfound periods of prosperity under Canute, who went on to eschew violent conquest in favour of a more temperate policy. It was during Canute's years in power that the relocation of the town's core to the area later enclosed by the town walls was consolidated. The infamous anecdote that Canute attempted to repel the tide at a Southampton shore is now considered by most historians to be the stuff of myth and legend. Nevertheless, both this tale and Canute's indisputable association with the town and surrounding area have seen his name given to roads and buildings for many years.

─────

The town's connection to the English monarch continued upon Canute's death in 1035, when another of Ethelred's sons, Edward, landed at the town on his return from France. He brought with him considerable forces, but did not become king until the death of Canute's son, Harthacnut, in 1042; he was known as Edward the Confessor. Edward died in 1066, and the witan chose Harold as his successor. Before the end of the year, William of Normandy attacked England, landing at Pevensey in East Sussex. Harold was killed at the ensuing Battle of Hastings. When William's invasion reached London it was met with submission rather than resistance, and he was formally made king at Westminster Abbey on Christmas Day, at the end of an especially eventful year.

In order to know what his newly acquired kingdom contained, William commissioned a huge inventory. The Domesday Book was completed and presented to him in 1086. It recorded that Southampton was populated by seventy-six 'original' householders, and that a further ninety-six had settled in the town since the Conquest. The new residents were divided into approximately two-thirds French and one-third English, and the area in which the former resided has been immortalised with the naming of French Street. Likewise there was also English Street, which was renamed High Street in the sixteenth century. In the post-Conquest period, the town was regarded as being split into two boroughs, each with its own church for the use of French or English worshippers. The French church, St Michael's, was built not long after the Conquest, and was named in honour of the patron saint of Normandy. There have been extensive adaptations over the years, such as the spire that now sits on the Norman tower, but many original features remain, especially internally.

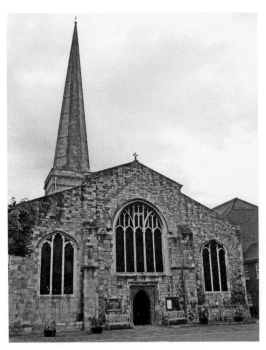

St Michael's church, 2011.

The Domesday record of Southampton omitted other residents of the town, however – specifically the poor or labouring class, who were seen as statistically irrelevant as they contributed nothing in taxation. William's grand itinerary, therefore, contains no absolute figure for Southampton's population in the late eleventh century, but around 1,000 can be considered a reasonable estimate. The town was thus not a great metropolis – Bristol was over three times larger and Winchester up to seven times – but it continued to enjoy a comparatively prosperous period. This affluence was common to a number of ports on the South Coast of England, as the links with William's homeland remained important. Southampton's geographical position was also significant, being approximately the same distance from London and Bristol, and a key point on the route between Normandy and Winchester.

Henry, the great-grandson of William the Conqueror, married Eleanor of Aquitaine in 1152, and two years later became the King of England upon the death of King Stephen. The marriage with Eleanor meant that in addition to the existing trade with Normandy, new commerce sprang up between England and vineyards in the Gascony area of south-west France. Southampton quickly became a prominent wine port, and the wine trade remained an important factor in the town's economy for several hundred years. Meanwhile, English beer on occasion travelled in the opposite direction. These business links with France, combined with Southampton's French population, meant that some merchants in the town (and possibly Winchester as well) were likely to have been bilingual.

From about this time, Southampton's defences were enhanced in accordance with its growing significance as a commercial port. As in a number of other towns, the Normans built a castle in Southampton after the Conquest, both as a signal of their power and as a base from which to maintain it. Since the monarchs of the time still oversaw kingdoms on both sides of the Channel, the town was a key embarkation point. The castle was located at the north end of Bull Street (today's Bugle Street), and subsequently gave its name to nearby Castle Lane. It was first mentioned in a document in 1153, but it is likely that a fortification on the site was originally built in the reign of William the Conqueror. This is suggested by the fact that coins from the era have been found at the location, and that the motte (the man-made earthen mound on which the castle was built) was large, consistent with others constructed soon after the Conquest. Furthermore, one of William's chief aides, William FitzOsbern, spent a good deal of time in Hampshire, and initiated the building of many castles throughout the country. His schemes sometimes made use of forced labour, and while FitzOsbern was successful in his endeavours, some of his methods have been brought into question.

The motte would have been surrounded by a ditch up to 65ft wide and a wooden fence, and originally the castle keep itself would also have been made of timber. Records show that between 1155 and 1162, over £50 was spent on building work at Southampton Castle, including the bridges of the castle and bailey, the chapel and the royal chamber, where the king and queen resided during their visits to the town. Henry II and Queen Eleanor were in Southampton in early 1157, as was the king on a number of occasions in this period while journeying to and from Normandy. In 1163, he was greeted upon his arrival in Southampton by Archbishop Thomas Becket, and eleven years later the king set out from the town on his pilgrimage to Canterbury to atone for Becket's murder.

Adjacent to the castle keep was the bailey – an enclosed area in which animals were kept and where the people could seek refuge if the town was attacked. This area was bounded by a wall that reached down to the seashore to the west

A remaining section of the castle bailey wall, built in the thirteenth or fourteenth century.

of the castle, where a dedicated quayside was built. By 1153, the Normans were building domestic houses in stone nearby; like the castle, some of them benefited from having their own quays for access to Southampton Water. Castle Quay was first documented in 1189, but the site has never been extensively excavated and now lies beneath Western Esplanade. It may have been made of both stone and wood, and adapted over the years. Southampton Water was quite shallow here, and it is likely that large, seagoing ships anchored some distance away and transferred their goods to the quay with smaller vessels.

Wine remained Southampton's primary import, still largely coming from the west and south-west of France, although Henry Englefield's assertion that the town enjoyed 'almost a monopoly of the French wine trade' was something of an overstatement. Wine was important to Henry II not only because of the taxes he levied on its arrival, but also because of his own need for large quantities of wine at his many banquets. One of the places in which the wine was stored when it was landed in Southampton was Castle Hall, the largest building relating to the castle that still stands, albeit badly ruined. The hall was originally built in the first half of the twelfth century and featured a timber floor between the two storeys, which were linked by a stone spiral staircase. The upper floor was a dwelling hall, while the ground floor served as storage for casks of wine. Early in the thirteenth century, the timber floor was replaced by a barrel vault made of stone, which has been partially restored and can be seen today. It may be that these alterations to the hall signified a change – or partial change – in its function, but this cannot be confirmed.

Just before the adaptations to Castle Hall were made, another building for storing wine was constructed: Castle Vault in Western Esplanade. The vault itself remains virtually intact – the only building relating to the castle to have done so – but originally it had a second storey, which has not survived. With just one door and one small window, the vault was extremely secure, and thus provided safe storage for the valuable wines.

The latter part of the twelfth century was evidently a time of intense construction in Southampton. As well as the ongoing development of the castle and its related satellite sites (nearly £150 was spent on the castle between 1191 and 1195, although it is not clear from surviving records exactly what work was carried out), the West Hall was constructed. Its owner was the prominent

Castle Vault, one of the few surviving buildings from the time of the castle, was used for storage and originally had an upper floor, which has long since gone.

Colloquially known as Canute's Palace, this Norman building near Town Quay was probably used as a storage facility.

Gervaise le Riche, a man as wealthy as his name suggests, who was involved in overseeing some of the works on the castle. Le Riche used the hall as his main residence, and after his death, it was occupied by various other great men of the town, who in turn made their own extensions and adaptations to it. Also in the late twelfth century, a large two-storey house was built in Porter's Lane at the southern end of the High Street. The house was of sufficient size and grandeur to be of considerable importance: Englefield described it as over 100ft in length and featuring a number of delicate carvings and impressive windows. Sadly, however, in the 200 years since Englefield's tour of the town, the ravages of time and the Second World War have taken their toll, and the building has now greatly deteriorated.

Southampton's domestic and residential buildings of this era were of timber construction, as evidenced by archaeological discoveries in the twentieth century.

Later, stone houses in the southern part of the town were found to have been erected on sites formerly occupied by wooden buildings. Fittings into which timber beams would have been placed were uncovered, as well as related finds that gave an indication of their age. The excavations also revealed the unavoidable dangers of timber construction: there was frequent evidence of fire, which diminished with the later increase in stone building.

≈≈ ≈≈

By the start of the thirteenth century, Southampton's port was ranked third in the country in terms of taxes levied there, trailing only Boston in Lincolnshire and London. This picture may not be completely accurate, however, since figures for Bristol and other ports in western England are unrecorded. But, within a couple of years a deterioration in trade with Normandy had a great impact on the town's commerce, which was partially assuaged by the still developing Gascony wine trade.

At the same time, protection of the town was becoming more important. The kings of the era – Richard I, John and Henry III – recognised the value of the town's trade and its strategic positioning. Additionally the king visited the town periodically and stayed at the castle, at which times security was paramount. The king travelled the country almost continually, residing at a castle for a time before moving on again. This policy kept the monarch prominent in the eyes of the people (and thus in control), and meant that no single town had the heavy burden of supporting him and his entourage on a permanent basis. Part of the expenditure on the castle that began in 1201 was used to 'carry timber from many places to Southampton Castle for the construction there of the king's houses', presumably in preparation for his next visit. According to the Victorian historian Revd J.S. Davies, King John 'was frequently at Southampton'.

Meanwhile the town's protection was enhanced by a large fence that surrounded the most densely populated area; the castle was a stronghold within a stronghold. Entry to the town was achieved through a number of gates, the primary one being the north gate, or Bargate, which was reached by a bridge over a large moat. It is likely that the Bargate was first built in the latter part of the twelfth century, replacing a section of timber stockade and featuring a portcullis protecting the large entry arch. Passage through the gate was manned by a representative of the town, who levied tolls on goods going in and out. Nevertheless, the town's finances were far from healthy: levies and other taxes paled in comparison with the cost of upgrading its defences. The situation became so acute that, in 1228, the men of Southampton had to 'plead their poverty' before the king.

The East Gate was constructed at around the same time as the Bargate, standing across what is now part of East Street. It was documented in 1217 (by which time Southampton was overseen by a mayor), and, while of equally sturdy build, was much smaller than the Bargate with a narrower entrance. Initially, however, the two important gates were joined not by a strong, stone wall but by an earthen rampart topped with a wooden fence. These rudimentary defences were gradually rebuilt in stone – the east wall in the vicinity of the East Gate was one of the first parts to be upgraded in about 1200. The East Gate took its place in a network of roads, providing access to and from the town through the eastern part of the stockade. It was at the far end of East Street, the only road of any size and significance to join English Street and the town walls to the east. It was densely populated with traders – a shopping street of great importance – and continued beyond the enclosed area, crossing the defensive ditch and progressing towards St Mary's church on the approximate site of the old, Saxon minster. At its western end, English (High) Street ran perpendicularly through the town from the Bargate in the north to the seafront.

For many years, however, English Street was blocked at its halfway point by Holy Rood church, which sat virtually in the middle of the road. The section of the street to the north of the church was mostly made up of small shops, while the southern end, which developed further following the Conquest, became populated with the homes of the town's merchants and the warehouses that their trade used. Later, in the fourteenth century, Holy Rood church was relocated marginally to the east (where its remains still stand), but the Audit House was constructed on the site. This building, in turn, was demolished in the late eighteenth century, when the thoroughfare was opened up along its entire length for the first time.

Southampton's streets were arranged on a grid pattern in much the same way as Hamwic. This layout became more defined in the early part of the thirteenth century as older timber dwellings were replaced with new stone buildings. Several street names betrayed the businesses found in their respective areas, such as Butcher Row, Brewhouse Lane and Market Lane. The thoroughfares that extended beyond both the East Gate and the Bargate gave rise to a small number of buildings constructed along the roadsides – what would become known as ribbon development many years later. In later years, these two roads

An eighteenth-century engraving of the East Gate, which was originally built in the twelfth century and led towards what is now the St Mary's area of the city.

came to be key axes in the future growth of the town. At around mid-century the general layout of Southampton had settled into a form that survived with little alteration for another 400 years.

Further beyond the walls were fields cultivated by the town's merchants, who often pursued domestic farming in addition to their overseas trading interests. By the eleventh century, the harbour on which Hamwic previously stood had silted up to the extent that the newly created piece of land (known as the Salt Marsh) could be used for farming. Inevitably, however, this area was prone to flooding, and, in 1228, the Common was appropriated from the northerly manor of Shirley. Additionally the Common lands directly outside the town walls – Hoglands, Houndwell, and East and West Marlands – were used for arable farming, providing the people with a great proportion of their food. Unusually, in comparison with many other towns, Southampton has managed to retain the vast majority of these common lands and they are now used as parks.

The Undercroft in Simnel Street is another excellent surviving example of Southampton's Norman architecture.

The town's wine trade continued and maintained an important role in royal circles. In the mid-1220s, wine was sent from Southampton to Corfe and Portchester castles, and, at the end of that decade, to Windsor. Benedict Ace, Mayor of Southampton for most of the 1240s, was primarily responsible for the handling of the king's wines locally, and Henry III himself later took great interest in those who would become Ace's successors. Undeniably, wine brought prosperity to the town, either directly or through related industries and services, and as the thirteenth century progressed, trading in wool developed alongside it. Indeed, the two were almost complementary – the primary import was wine and wool became the leading export – and between them, they constituted the bulk of Southampton's economic activity. The wool trade flourished in the reign of Edward I, who succeeded Henry III in 1272. English wool at the time was becoming renowned as the finest in Europe and was in great demand across the Continent. It was shipped to north-east and south-west France, the Atlantic coast of Spain and the Netherlands. As a result of these links Southampton hosted merchants from all these countries and more, giving the town a cosmopolitan character.

Archaeological discoveries in recent years give a fascinating insight into the life of a typical merchant of this era. The site of the dwelling occupied by Richard of Southwick (in Cuckoo Lane, near the town wall at West Quay) reveals much about his life through the household items and waste discovered there. Although not excessively wealthy, Richard lived well, as a businessman dealing in wine, wool and potentially other goods. He used expensive imported ceramic ware at his table, including desirable items sourced from Spain and France. Some of his diet was also imported, such as grapes and figs, but otherwise it comprised foodstuffs only available to men of a certain level of income – mutton, beef, oysters and mussels. Other evidence shows that the women at Richard's home were likely to have been involved in sewing or weaving, enhancing his entrepreneurial position yet further.

Commerce in Southampton both allowed and necessitated new buildings, such as the Weigh House in French Street. It was constructed in about 1280, as evidenced by the style of its windows, and, as with many of the town's buildings, was altered over the ensuing years. The Weigh House was home to the king's weigh beam: the family of the Earl of Warwick was charged with weighing the town's imports and exports.

As trade prospered, Italian merchants sought to maximise their profits by excluding Flemish distributors and beginning to deal directly with English ports. Initially, they traded through London and other ports further north on the east coast, but, in 1305, a vessel from Genoa docked at Southampton and thereafter more followed suit. Fourteen years later, five Venetian galleys arrived at the port, but the townspeople, fuelled by xenophobic outrage on account of dispensations offered to the Italians by the English monarchs, were less than welcoming. Fights with the Venetian crews erupted and riotous exchanges ensued, with both sides suffering casualties. The Italians soon retreated to their ships, taking all available spoils, and leaving the town in a considerably worse condition.

Threats also came from much closer to home than the Mediterranean. In September 1321, a fleet from Winchelsea approached the port to burn the ships docked there. Despite being offered two ships if they would take their leave, the men continued their destruction the following day. After these incidents the people of Southampton were, probably justifiably, wary of any unexpected arrivals in the port, but especially of Italian visitors – who were seen as a threat regardless of their actual intentions. In 1322, a ship from Genoa arrived at the port to shelter from rough seas, and the townspeople exacted their revenge for the events of three years earlier on the innocent crew. But trade with Italy was so valuable that the following year Edward II intervened, and at his behest the mayor called a truce. Despite this, it was two decades before Southampton's trade with Italy recovered, in which time the town's fortunes worsened before they improved.

The newfound vigilance towards potential threats at least focused attention on upgrading the town walls, castle and defences in general. In early 1326, the town burgesses petitioned the king for additional funds, stating that they had 'spent heavily already on the work', and Edward responded by granting permission for them to exact a levy of a penny in every pound's worth of goods passing through the town gates in either direction. But good intentions were not followed up with worthwhile actions, and there was little evidence of new projects. Edward III succeeded his murdered father in 1327, and eleven years later must have wished that rather more attention had been paid to the protection of Southampton.

SOUTHAMPTON'S MAYORS – THE FIRST 100 YEARS

Although the role of Mayor of Southampton was mentioned in records early in the thirteenth century, the names of those serving are lost until 1237. The following is a list of mayoral appointments for the ensuing century with known dates in which they took office. Many of the names reflect the French element in the town's population during this period.

1237	Benedict
1247	Benedict
1248	Benedict
1260 & 1262	unknown
1270	Simon de la Bolehuge
1284	Robert le Mercier
1286	John de Bynedon
1288	Robert le Mercier
1290	unknown
1291	Robert le Barbyr
1294	Thomas le Blunde
1295	Robert le Mercier
1298	Robert le Barbyr
1300	John de Schyerlye
1303	Adam le Horder
1311	John de Schyerlye
1313	Hugo Sampson
1315	Henry de Lym
1316	Thomas de Bynedon
1317	Richard de Barefluet
1318	Hugo Sampson
1319	John le Flemynge
1320	Henry de Lym
1321	Richard Forst
1323	Hugo Sampson
1324	Thomas de Bynedon
1326	Walter de Brakkelye
1328	Roger Norman
1329	Henry de Lym
1330	Roger Norman
1331	Thomas de Bynedon
1332	Nicholas de Mondenard
1333	Hugo Sampson
1334	Lawrence de Mees
1336	Thomas de Bynedon

three

RANSACK & RECOVERY

I f English relations with Italy were strained, those with France were rapidly approaching breaking point. In 1337, the French throne became vacant and conflict arose over the right to the title of King of France: the French house of Valois staked its claim and the Plantagenets of England (being of French descent from the time following the Norman Conquest) did likewise. The south-west territories of Aquitaine and Gascony, so closely linked with Southampton through the wine trade, were already allied to the English, while Flanders, on the north-west border, soon also displayed its sympathies towards Edward III.

Raids on English towns along the Channel were not uncommon in this era, even in times of peace, but with the outbreak of what was later known as the Hundred Years War the attacks became more focused and strategic. Portsmouth was targeted in March 1338 and afterwards the Channel Islands, with inhabitants killed and buildings looted and burnt. The people of Southampton would have been aware of these raids and may even have heard of the specific threat to their own town: the French commander Hugh Quiéret made no secret of the monetary rewards offered to 'the first man to breach the defences of Southampton'.

If warnings were received they went unheeded, and ships intended to patrol the waters of the Solent failed to materialise. French forces attacked Southampton on the morning of Sunday, 5 October 1338, when most of the townspeople were in church and entirely unsuspecting of their impending fate. The French arrived in around fifty galleys, together with some Genoese, who must barely have required the financial incentives offered by the French to join the raids: the injustice of 1322 still rankled and the Italians needed little encouragement to bring suffering upon the people of Southampton.

At this time, it must be remembered, there were no defensive walls along the shores of Southampton as the water was considered protection enough, but the

A mid-nineteenth century lithograph of St Michael's church, which was 'polluted by the effusion of blood and by homicide' in the infamous French raid of 1338.

folly of this policy was swiftly borne out in spectacular style. The fleet landed and the invaders quickly made their way into the town, at which point a number of the locals fled to the countryside. The townspeople who remained had some success in repelling the initial attacks, but were unable to contain the assault that followed. The French and Italians swept through the streets, 'slaughtering the townsfolk in their houses or as they came tumbling out of the churches'. Being the primary point of ingress, the south-westerly area of the town was one of the worst affected. Wooden buildings were burnt, including those adjacent to St Michael's church, the Frenchmen being either unaware or unconcerned that the church had been founded by their own ancestors. The sacrilege to the holy building was considered so great that the following year St Michael's was reconsecrated by the Bishop of Sarum.

With the locals apparently unable to offer any worthwhile resistance, the Frenchmen and their allies set about pillaging the town. Houses and shops were looted, women raped and innocent civilians hanged in their homes. So confident were the invaders that no one would hinder their exploits that they decided to stay for the night, but this bravado proved to be their downfall. Some of the townspeople who had managed to evade the marauding Frenchmen and escape Southampton raised the alarm, and a retaliatory force was put together consisting of men from the surrounding areas. They repelled those invaders who had lingered in the town, and several hundred were killed before they could reach the safety of their ships. Later, but based on a contemporary account, historian John Stow related an anecdote of a Sicilian prince who during the clashes shouted 'Rancon!', meaning 'ransom', to indicate that he was willing to pay to be spared from imminent death. His opponent, however, misheard the prince's cry as 'Francon', an apparent admission that he was a Frenchman, and there the brief conversation violently ended.

The fleeing French and Italians managed to set fire to various parts of the town en route to their ships, but one of the most disastrous days in Southampton's history was not yet over. With the greatest of ironies, the forces assembled in the nearby countryside to drive the invaders from the town decided to help themselves to the remaining spoils. Large quantities of wool due for export had been left unburnt by the raiders, but it was soon carried away. Many of the townspeople lay dead, their former homes ransacked and burning. The large Italian merchants abandoned the port, some never to return; two prominent companies from Florence temporarily relocated their business to Bristol. During the next year, Southampton's trade dwindled to almost nothing, with no wool exports whatsoever leaving the town. The four months immediately following the raid saw a pitifully low customs income of less than £8. In less than two days, Southampton had been transformed from a prosperous, bustling port into a ruin.

For many years, there has been a theory that one or more members of the Grimaldi family were involved in the 1338 raid and that the spoils of their endeavours were subsequently used in the development of Monaco. However, their presence at the raid is in question. It has also been suggested that the Grimaldis took their loot to Eze, a small French town to the west of Monaco. With no firm evidence to support either of these stories, whether they are truth or myth may never be known.

The calamitous events of October 1338 had a profound impact not only on the town itself but also on the country. The invasion was seen as an embarrassment to the king and his realm, and the local people who had suffered and died were in some quarters considered to have failed in their duty of defending the kingdom. Shortly afterwards, the poet, Laurence Minot, composed an ode that recorded the incident for posterity, asserting that the people of Southampton did not surrender as meekly as others portrayed. Only a few days after the assault, meanwhile, Edward III commissioned the Earl of Arundel to conduct an enquiry into the disaster. The earl theorised that some of the town's keepers had helped to facilitate the attack, in that they 'neglected entirely to provide for the defence of parts threatened'.

Edward was, predictably, further enraged to learn of the looting that had taken place after the raid and urged the earl to name those at fault. The investigations lasted almost a year, and in the summer of 1339 culminated in the incarceration of customs collector, Nicholas de Moundenard, in the Tower of London. While he perhaps did not completely fulfil the role of scapegoat that the king may have wished upon him, the enquiries did Nicholas no favours, revealing considerable financial misappropriations. The same year the king visited the town himself, undoubtedly still smarting from the shame of the raid and the loss of his property in the associated looting. He inspected the defences and decreed that improvements should be made. The attack had shown that the castle offered no protection to the town and little sanctuary to its people in a time of crisis. It had been in poor condition as far back as 1246, when some of the townspeople were punished with fines for selling stone and wood from the crumbling building.

The king's view was shared by Thomas de Beauchamp, the Earl of Warwick, who would have an eventful military career as a commander in the Hundred Years War. He also visited in 1339, and was greatly unimpressed by what he found; in his estimation, Southampton was incapable of withstanding an invasion from as few as 200 men. On the basis of the two royal assessments, specific instructions were given that the southern and western shores of the town were to be walled, meaning that Southampton would be entirely enclosed. The castle, to which no renovations were made other than a few basic repairs after the French raid, would thus become a secondary, rather than a primary, defensive structure.

Although the work would not begin for a few years, the town was at times used as a military base. In May 1345, Henry of Lancaster's army was assembled there, setting sail for France in over 100 ships. Southampton, in fact, as revealed in a survey conducted that year, supplied a significant proportion of the king's vessels. The fleet was split into north and south sections. In the southern area, London naturally provided the most ships and men (twenty-five and 662 respectively), but Southampton almost matched these figures with twenty-one men and 576 ships. Portsmouth, by comparison, sent just five ships and less than 100 men. The following year, 1346, the men who would win a famous victory at Crécy also gathered at the town and left from the port. To assist with Southampton's protection in the meantime the keeper of arms at the Tower of London was instructed to provide new supplies of weapons. A number of guardians were appointed by the king to oversee the town's defences, and in many cases, auxiliary soldiers and archers were made available to them.

Trade (and thus general prosperity) did not improve, however, and two years later further hardship befell both the town and the whole country with the advent of the Black Death. Southampton was not as badly affected as other towns – almost a quarter of the inhabitants succumbed to the plague – but had it not been for the French attack a decade earlier, the population and, therefore, the death toll would surely have been greater. The thriving port of Bristol, by comparison, is thought to have been one of the first sizeable settlements to fall victim to the Black Death, with nearly half the townspeople dead in less than a year. The disease forced families to abandon their infected children to save the healthy and bodies were unceremoniously disposed of in mass graves, or 'plague pits'.

As the dark days of the plague began to recede, attention returned to the strengthening of Southampton's defences. Over the next fifty years, much money was devoted to extending and upgrading first the town's walls and later the castle. A tax levied specifically to fund the rebuilding of the walls (known as a 'murage') had been in place since soon after the French raid, and, in the summer of 1355, it was renewed. This meant that all goods leaving or entering the town, whether by road or sea, were taxed in order to contribute to the new defences. In about 1360, the West Wall was built, partially made up of the frontages of existing stone houses and reinforced to a thickness of 3ft. Despite the greatly improved security this work effected, some of the residents were initially reluctant to forego direct access to the waterfront. Added in front of the wall was an arcade consisting of a series of tall arches, a number of which remain today. On top of the wall and arcade was a parapet and rampart walk, featuring gaps in the stonework through which defending forces were able to drop stones (or other useful deterrents) on potential attackers below.

In 1369, further work was deemed necessary and additional taxes were imposed on the townspeople in line with their means. But seven years later, many had tired of the extra financial burden and left Southampton, with some of those remaining ready to follow. The wisdom of upgrading the defences was soon borne out, however, when the French attacked again – only to be repelled without breaching the town.

The arcade and part of the west wall (c.1900).

One of the largest remaining sections of the old town walls – Western Esplanade, 2011.

In the aftermath of the attempted invasion and with the war against France still ongoing, the role of Southampton Castle was reassessed. It was considered important and strategic enough to warrant the investment that would strengthen it sufficiently against further attacks, and work began in 1378. This was the first significant attention paid to its upkeep for nearly a century, and it was bolstered by the presence of a garrison of around 300 men. Two prominent master masons of the time, William Wynford and Henry Yevele, were taken on. Wynford had worked on Windsor Castle and Wells Cathedral, while Yevele, the most prolific and successful stonemason of his era, had been employed at the Tower of London and Westminster Abbey. Construction lasted several years, with workers brought in from neighbouring counties and as far afield as Somerset and Oxfordshire. The project was overseen by Sir John Arundel, the governor of the castle, whose name was subsequently given to the tower at the north-west corner of the town walls.

The castle keep was almost completely redesigned over the course of the next few years, probably in a style consistent with other contemporary castle works. It featured a number of turrets affording views across Southampton Water, and around the keep were a secondary defensive wall and a ditch. Improvements were also made to the castle gates, but of the four gates renovated at the time, only two are visible today. The Watergate in the western wall led to the quayside, and is still in very good condition. The castle's East Gate (not to be confused with the town gate in East Street), is greatly ruined, however: all that remains are a few steps and the bases of the towers that would have flanked the narrow entrance passage. Such gates were generally built with a narrow opening to ensure that they were easier to defend; the inconvenience of slowing down traffic as it passed through the gate was considered a worthwhile sacrifice if it enhanced the castle's security.

Between 1378 and 1388, a total of nearly £2,000 was spent on the castle, the majority of it in the first two years. With renovations to castle and walls complete, Southampton had been transformed from a town of desolation and ruin after the raids of 1338 to one of the strongest fortresses in the country. The walls entirely enclosed the town, standing at some points as high as 30ft. Seven heavily guarded gates gave access to the settlement within, and there were an additional twenty-nine towers acting as observational and weaponry positions.

The completion of Southampton's new defences coincided, somewhat ironically, with a low ebb in terms of population – estimated at less

Castle Watergate, seen here in about 1930, was the primary route into the castle for deliveries landed at the nearby quayside.

than 2,000 – and a hiatus in the conflict with France. During this period, though, the seeds were sown for the recovery of the town's economy. The Gascony wine trade was reinvigorated and so, perhaps more significantly, was the Italian wool trade. Once more Southampton's geographical position counted in its favour: the Italians required a port well linked to both London and the Cotswolds, which supplied some of the finest wool available. Additionally, their preferred port was ideally on the Channel, giving easy access to the Netherlands, which Italian ships also frequented. After discounting London itself and finding the harbour facilities at Sandwich inferior, the Italians settled on Southampton.

They were further encouraged by an Act of Parliament of 1378, by which merchants were allowed to land their goods and load others at Southampton for the same customs payments as would have been exacted at Calais, their more regular destination. Genoese and Venetian traders thus benefited from shorter (and therefore cheaper) voyages, while Southampton became what has been described as 'the centre of all the Levant trade of the kingdom'. The Levant was the name given to a large area of the north-west portion of the

Above The Wool House, as its name suggests, was used for storing wool prior to export. In recent years, it has been home to the city's maritime museum.

Left Much admired; the impressively engineered roof of the Wool House remains largely as it was originally built in the fourteenth century.

The Bargate Guildhall was for many years used as a meeting place and later served as a local history museum.

Arabian Peninsula, approximately comprising today's Syria, Israel and Jordan. In the fourteenth century, this region became an important trading centre, exporting and importing goods from Europe and the Far East, and producing other commodities locally. Ships from elsewhere in the Mediterranean also began to reappear in Southampton, and for a time trade was as robust as it ever had been.

This revitalisation was reflected in the construction and extensive use of the Wool House, one of Southampton's finest medieval buildings, which to this day overlooks Southampton Water at the southern end of the city. The Wool House was built in the fourteenth century and, as its name suggests, was used as a warehouse in which wool was kept before being shipped; hence its proximity to the shore. Although the building has been somewhat altered over the centuries, key original features remain, particularly the side walls, south-facing main door and the impressive roof. As the fourteenth century became the fifteenth, other building work was also occurring in the town, notably renovations to the Bargate. It was around this time that the new north front of the gate was constructed, and soon afterwards, the main room on the first floor became the Guildhall. The room was named after its use for meetings of the Guild Merchant, and it hosted a wide variety of functions well into the twentieth century.

⁂

Hostilities with France were renewed when Henry V came to the throne in 1413. Southampton again took on a more military role and in doing so its commerce suffered a little. Most famously, it served as the point of muster and departure for the forces bound for Agincourt in 1415. Early that year, the king's ship, *Holy Ghost*, was renovated in Southampton and there was an ongoing flurry of shipbuilding. Henry evidently recognised the advantages of using the port as a departure point from which he might take an army to France, as Edward III had done seventy years earlier. Although many of the supplies needed were kept in the Tower of London and the capital's port provided adequate facilities, the surrounding area was far from ideal for assembling a large number of troops. The outskirts of Southampton, however, were suitable for such accommodation, and the town itself was well defended. Furthermore, local sailors were well versed in crossing the Channel. By the middle of May, ships were being accumulated at Southampton and two months later, the king arrived in the town. At the end of the month, thousands of troops were pouring into the area, together with cattle, for food on the campaign, and other supplies, including bows and arrows and armour. At the same time, the king wrote an ultimatum to his French counterpart, Charles VI, which was issued from Southampton, and urged Charles to 'give us what we are owed and by the will of the Almighty avoid a deluge of human blood'.

As the departure for France drew near, Henry stayed at Titchfield Abbey on several occasions, but while preparations were still in progress, a plot against him was discovered, perpetrated by Richard, Earl of Cambridge, Lord Henry Scrope and Sir Thomas Grey. The three men planned a coup in which Henry would be deposed and replaced by the Earl of March, cousin of the Earl of Cambridge. The reasons behind the conspiracy are not entirely clear, and may never be, but a motive might have been revenge against the earlier actions of Henry IV, who, ten years earlier, had ordered the execution of Scrope's uncle, the Archbishop of York. Another theory is that French financial persuasion might have encouraged the plotters in their plans. Whatever the truth about their motivations, the conspirators were undone when the Earl of March visited the king at Portchester Castle and revealed their intentions.

The three men were arrested and incarcerated in Southampton Castle. On 2 August 1415, after an enquiry lasting two days, Cambridge, Scrope and Grey were charged with high treason, specifically 'consenting to destroy and kill the present lord king'. Cambridge and Grey confessed their guilt, and the latter was sentenced to death and executed that very day, led through the town to the Bargate where he was publicly beheaded. Exercising their legal right, Cambridge and Scrope elected to be tried by their peers. This presented little difficulty, since the majority of their peers were also gathered in Southampton, ready to depart for France.

According to popular local legend the location of the hearing was the Red Lion Inn on the High Street, although it is perhaps more likely to have been the main hall in the castle. The trials took place on 5 August, and the nineteen assembled peers unanimously found Cambridge and Scrope guilty as charged. Their punishment was exacted as swiftly as Grey's; they were executed the same day. Since the Earl of Cambridge was a member of the royal family, the king spared him the ignominy of being hanged and drawn, settling instead for a simple beheading. Scrope, meanwhile, was dragged the length of the town to the Bargate, where the same ultimate fate awaited him: on Henry's orders, his severed head was later displayed on York's city gates. A plot that could have jeopardised the entire Agincourt campaign had been quashed, but its notoriety led to its prominent inclusion in Shakespeare's *Henry V*.

Less than a week after the deaths of Cambridge and Scrope, the king left for France to lead his men to one of the most famous victories in English history.

The increase in military activity in Henry's reign saw further efforts made to improve Southampton's defences. Foremost among the enhancements was the construction of God's House Tower at the south-east corner of the town walls – a sturdy and imposing three-storey structure offering protection to the sluices through which flowed the water used in the town's moat. It adjoined God's House Gate, which had been built around a century earlier and boasted two portcullises for potential invaders to contend with. Both the gate and the subsequent tower took their names from the nearby God's House Hospital, founded towards the end of the twelfth century by Gervaise le Riche, who had built and lived in the West Hall. Adjoining the hospital was a chapel, which became the burial place of the Earl of Cambridge following his execution. Once completed, the new tower acted as a store for weaponry and was the workplace of the town gunner, an important and highly paid civic official tasked with the manufacture of gunpowder and repairs to the town's arms. The castle,

God's House Tower, the bastion at the south-easterly corner of the town walls, was, like the Bargate, used as a prison for some of its life.

however, was gradually seen as less important. Despite enormous expenditure on renovations in the 1370s and '80s, and despite the king's not infrequent visits, the town's former stronghold was neglected for many years to come.

Henry V continued his enthusiastic shipbuilding policy: new vessels were made and older ones were renovated both in Southampton and at nearby Hamble. The programme was partially overseen by William Soper, who had worked on the fleet for the Agincourt campaign and was also mayor of the town on two occasions. Of particular note was the *Anne*, which was launched in the town in 1416 and was fitted with two masts; no records survive of such a vessel being built earlier. One ship that was built at this time, however, never fulfilled the role for which she was designed. *Grace Dieu*, weighing at least 1,400 tons, was the largest ship in Henry's impressive new navy when she was completed in 1418, and no larger ship was built in England for over 200 years. But *Grace Dieu* only ever completed one voyage (a short but arduous journey to the Isle of Wight, during which her disgruntled crew threatened rebellion), and the ship's career ended before it had truly begun: she was towed up the Hamble river, where she lay for nearly twenty years until she was struck by lightning and virtually destroyed. Many of the wreck's remaining timbers were plundered, but the outline of the ship continued to be visible at low tides well into the twentieth century. Extensive archaeological explorations took place on the site as recently as 2004.

The brief boom in Southampton's shipbuilding industry may have helped to line the pockets of such entrepreneurial individuals as Soper, but the economy of the town as a whole saw little benefit. Any further prosperity that might have accrued was curtailed by the death of Henry V in 1422. Some of the ships intended for his navy became commercial vessels, while others never took to the seas again.

In almost 500 years since the brief career and fiery demise of *Grace Dieu*, the wreck of the ship has been the subject of continued interest. The first phase of this was practical rather than archaeological: very soon after her destruction, any remaining useable wood was removed from her carcass and used elsewhere. Thereafter, the ship was largely untouched until the late nineteenth century when more timbers were salvaged; some of these are now kept by Winchester Museums. The pieces of wood reveal a great deal about the construction of the vessel, particularly that it was done roughly and quickly with little allowance for fine details.

In the 1930s, the wreck was examined again, and, in 1970, it was purchased by the University of Southampton. Ten years later, more investigations were undertaken, this time by the Archaeological Research Centre at the National Maritime Museum; these continued until 1985. Since then the university's Centre for Maritime Archaeology has persevered with work at the site, sometimes in conjunction with other bodies, including the Mary Rose Trust. In 2004, the centre joined forces with the Channel 4 television programme, *Time Team*, to revisit the wreck and use some of the latest archaeological technology. The stern of the ship was excavated and ultimately the data collected from the entire site was used to create a three-dimensional digital image of the remainder of the wreck, buried beneath the riverbed.

four

EUROPEAN TRADE

I n 1445, Southampton welcomed Margaret of Anjou, Henry VI's bride-to-be, on her arrival before their wedding. She spent one April night in Portsmouth and then journeyed by water to Southampton the next day, residing at the God's House Hospital. After a delay of four days – possibly due to illness on her part – Margaret met Henry in the town and they were married in Titchfield, by the Bishop of Salisbury, the following week.

That summer, the king bestowed a charter of incorporation upon the town. This formalised the roles of the mayor and bailiffs, who were to be elected annually on the Friday before St Matthew's Day (21 September). Subsequently, as the town's economic fortunes improved, so too did the ability of its leaders to control its commercial destiny, and, two years later, further significant changes to the governance of the town took place. Until this time, edicts issued by the Sheriff of Hampshire had naturally taken effect in Southampton, but they were not always warmly received by the town's merchants. The charter of 1447 created the 'County of the town of Southampton' (which included Portsmouth), with its own sheriff – who was presumably more sympathetic towards local issues.

Before long, the governance of Southampton settled into an established model, which lasted for several centuries. Previously, the dominant administrative body had been the Guild Merchant, assembled from prominent and powerful local businessmen, whose successes and failures were often reflected in the prosperity of the town. Guild members were, naturally, distinguished from lay townspeople by their occupations: they were merchants, lawyers, shipowners and wholesalers, as opposed to labourers and craftsmen. About fifty or sixty of these professionals became the burgesses of the borough Corporation, of whom less than twenty were elected by the burgesses to make up the earliest form of the Council. This body included the mayor and six or so former mayors, known as aldermen, who also acted as the justices of the town.

They were assisted by a legal expert (the Recorder), the sheriff and two bailiffs. It was within this group that the true power lay in terms of the town's governance and administration, which now involved maintenance of Corporation property and control of its finances. The fact that members of the Corporation were not elected by the people of Southampton quickly led to what has been described as a self-interested alliance. Burgesses and aldermen contrived to appoint each other to the positions of municipal power, even including the nominations of the town's two members of Parliament. This (at best) flawed system was perpetuated for many years, as it was in many other corporations around the country. When the Council or its decisions were challenged, its members simply closed ranks.

Their meeting place was a building known as the Audit House, located in the middle of the town's main High Street. The site was occupied by Holy Rood church until 1320, when it moved to its current position and the Audit House was built in its place soon afterwards. Southampton's governors used the first floor, with the mayor and aldermen holding a weekly meeting every Friday in the room that housed the town's ancient records and official weights and measures. Larger meetings were held at the more capacious Guildhall in the Bargate. The ground floor of the Audit House, meanwhile, became home to some of the town's markets and this arrangement remained virtually unchanged for several hundred years.

<hr />

The Hundred Years War finally drew to a close in 1453, with the vast majority of English land in France reverting to French rule. It was suspected that the southern coast of England was to become a target for attack once more, with the French ebullient in their victory and keen to remind the English of their defeat. In 1457, just such a foray did indeed occur, but this time the people and defences of Southampton were well prepared. Lookouts had been sent to Portsmouth and Lepe, and intelligence from other nearby localities also filtered back. Thus forewarned, the town was able to make speedy improvements to the walls and gates, and additional soldiers were drafted in from Salisbury. Mercifully, these measures were ultimately not called into action: the French vessels that ventured up Southampton Water and approached the town were repelled by gunfire, and the settlement was not threatened. Frustrated, the attackers turned their attention to Sandwich, which they invaded with a force of several thousand men, burning most of the town to the ground.

That same year Venetian ships were welcomed to Southampton. Having visited the port irregularly over the previous twenty years, the Venetians began to use it as the centre of their English trade, relocating from the capital. Affluent Italian merchants had become the subject of Londoners' envy, and tension erupted in a number of violent exchanges in 1456. As a result, the merchants departed London en masse, bound for Southampton and Winchester. But after requesting that several grand houses in Winchester be repaired in readiness for their occupancy, they instead opted to move directly to Southampton, thus enraging the Winchester landlords who had paid for the renovation of the mansions. London's (and Winchester's) loss was Southampton's gain and the Italians continued to trade from the town for several decades. The port facilities they used had recently been improved: a rudimentary crane had been installed by 1450, which, although powered and manoeuvred by hand, allowed larger and more cumbersome shipments to be processed. The mere presence of this crane confirms Southampton's commercial prominence at the time, as it was one of very few outside London.

In time, however, the nature of the town's commerce began to shift and trade with Italy fell away. A number of factors contributed to this, not least the conflicts that raged between the Italian states in the second half of the fifteenth century. This civil unrest was aptly mirrored by the Wars of the Roses, in which the competing houses of Lancaster and York did battle for more than thirty years over the right to the English throne. As might be imagined, international trading between two countries that were both fighting among themselves proved difficult. Additionally, the English saw an opportunity to achieve greater profits by using their own ships to travel to and from the Mediterranean, and thus compete on their own terms. To compound matters, relations between the French and the Venetians were less than harmonious in the late fifteenth century, and Italian ships were regularly attacked as they navigated the Channel and approached the South Coast of England. Southampton's fluctuating trade with Italy had peaked and declined for the last time.

Before the final visits of the Italian merchants in the early sixteenth century, Southampton's trade was already moving in new directions. A staple of metals was created at the town in 1492, during the reign of Henry VII, which meant that by royal recommendation it became a primary point of export for metals; it was authorised to conduct trade in this group of commodities, at the expense of other ports that had done so previously. Chief among the metals passing through Southampton was tin, which had been traded in the town since the middle of the fifteenth century, when Henry VI commandeered tin in the port to pay for his army. By the end of the century, an annual shipment arrived in Southampton from Cornwall, transported in a fleet of vessels.

It was also around this time that the seeds of Southampton's specialisation in merchant shipping were sown. In 1495, Henry VII built a dry dock in Portsmouth and from that time onwards the focus there was on the warships of the monarch's navy. Although warships would still be built in Southampton from time to time, the division between the military and merchant branches of the navy has largely remained.

The town and port still saw sporadic episodes of military action, since Britain was at times drawn into continuing European conflicts. In May 1512, the Marquis of Dorset, Thomas Grey (grandfather of Lady Jane Grey), assembled an army of 10,000 men at Southampton, to assist the Spanish king, Ferdinand, in his battles against the French. Henry VIII came to the town to inspect the troops. The king visited again the following year and, at his behest, repairs and improvements were made to the town walls and defences.

The decline in the numbers of Italian ships using the port at Southampton did not mean that Anglo-Italian trade as a whole was following the same downward spiral. Some Italian merchants retained their residences in Southampton and local businessmen cultivated close working relationships with them, gaining valuable insights into business practices and learning about European tastes in furniture and fashion. English merchants became increasingly adventurous and continued to send their own ships to the Mediterranean, securing significant business in sweet wines and currants. They were able to build grand houses that suited their growing affluence, and by far the most significant surviving example is the Tudor House, located opposite St Michael's church. It was constructed in either the late fifteenth or early sixteenth century by Sir John Dawtrey of Petworth and incorporated parts of the medieval building that previously occupied the site. Dawtrey was a customs official, also serving as Southampton's Member of Parliament and later as Sheriff of Hampshire. It seems likely that Tudor House was at some point inhabited by the prominent merchant Henry Huttoft, since John Leland (who traversed the country writing a history-cum-travelogue for Henry VIII) mistakenly opined that Huttoft had built it rather than Dawtrey. The house itself is a supreme example of Tudor architecture, featuring a banqueting hall with oak panelling and a fine ornamental garden. It has been sympathetically restored over the years and is now one of the city's museums.

The ships that wealthy merchants employed on the Mediterranean routes were variously owned – some by the Southampton businessmen themselves and others by the crown, which in turn were hired out. However, the great majority of the vessels were controlled by London merchants. These Londoners were not just involved in Mediterranean interests: they also dealt with Cornish tin and the resurgent Gascony wine trade, often to the detriment of Southampton businessmen. Nevertheless, the town's prosperous economy was strong enough to withstand an outbreak of the plague in 1519. Three years later, the Holy Roman Emperor, Charles V visited, departing from the port after meeting Henry VIII in Winchester. Queen Catherine of Aragon also came to the town in the mid-1520s, when Henry Huttoft was mayor.

Arguably, the seeds of Southampton's economic demise were sown in this decade, when Henry VIII's naval campaigns disrupted trade in the Channel and customs income in the town fell accordingly. To compound the situation, London merchants were exempt from making customs payments, so that much of the little trading that did take place failed to make any contribution to the town's finances. By the 1530s, the face of English shipping and commerce was changing rapidly. Trade itself was becoming more centred on London, not least because advances in shipbuilding and pilotage made negotiation of the Thames a much simpler prospect than before.

Additionally there was a decline in the export of wool to Italy and a counter-acting upturn in the cloth trade. Since the cloth markets were already based in London and wares were primarily bound for Holland and central Europe, merchants naturally preferred to export from the capital itself, rather than add unnecessary expense and delay by continuing to use Southampton. They with-drew from the town and returned to London, and to make matters even more desperate, took with them the other branches of trade that they had devel-oped on the south coast. One of the worst losses was the Cornish tin trade: the fleet made its last annual visit to Southampton in 1531, by which time the Corporation was virtually insolvent.

The situation deteriorated yet further. Henry Huttoft's daughter, Dorothy, had married a Florentine merchant named Antonio Guidotti: the social net-working that had facilitated such prosperous times even extended to the conjunction of families. Guidotti's business interests had initially been very suc-cessful; certainly in 1534 the relationship between father and son-in-law must have been a happy one, since Huttoft (in his second tenure as mayor) made Guidotti a burgess of the town. Perhaps, though, it was at this point that the bad omens began to appear. Guidotti's status as burgess was quashed, since Huttoft had made the decision 'without consent', and the Italian was considered 'a stranger'. In fact, it soon became apparent that Guidotti's affairs were far from being in order. His public image as a dependable, affluent merchant was a veneer covering the enormous debts he had accrued. In 1535, he disappeared and his creditors turned their attentions to Huttoft, whose world and wealth crumbled beneath him. A number of Southampton's other merchants had also relied on Guidotti's (supposed) business acumen and contacts in Italy, and as the truth became clear they too suffered the consequences.

The 1540s, therefore, were not a happy time in the commercial life of Southampton: in the first half of the decade average annual customs receipts were over 90 per cent lower than at their peak about thirty-five years earlier. As desperation set in the Corporation even borrowed money from wealthier townspeople, presumably those unaffected by Guidotti's misadventures. But, in 1543, as the repayments drew closer, war with France erupted once more and the town's little remaining trade declined yet further. A section of Southampton's younger inhabitants (and wise merchants) departed the town, bound for the more prosperous economic climate of London. In 1545, the Isle of Wight came under attack from French forces, but the mainland was not breached and, at approximately the end of the decade, the beautiful spire of St Mary's church was demolished to prevent potential invaders from using it as a navigational marker. Henry VIII's foresight in constructing defences eight years earlier at Calshot Castle (on the south-western coast of the Southampton estuary) appeared to have been well placed.

The government evidently became aware of Southampton's decaying economy and accordingly reduced its demands for financial contributions in 1552. Furthermore, Henry VIII's infamous spat with Rome was liable to infuriate the powerful French and Spanish Catholics, making the maintenance of strategically placed fortified towns all the more important. The rapid expansion of London had left many provincial towns trailing in its wake, and the Crown began to realise that they could be neglected no longer. Additionally there was public image to think of – particularly the perception of England held by other heads of Europe. Potential conflict was put aside in July 1554 when Philip of Spain arrived at Southampton, and was greeted by his bride-to-be, Mary Tudor. They were married in Winchester Cathedral just two days later.

Only two years earlier, Edward VI had visited the town, and described it as 'handsome, and for the bigness of it as fair houses as be in London'; but its impressive appearance was probably superficially applied for his benefit. By 1554, Southampton was 'in a state of dangerous decay', and Philip of Spain must have been somewhat shocked at the deteriorating condition of what was supposedly one of the premier ports on the English Channel. Mary may well have shared this opinion, but she was won over by the greetings given to her and her future husband by the people of Southampton. She rewarded the town by issuing a charter giving it a virtual monopoly on the import of malmsey wines and sweet wines from Crete and the Levant. These wines were to be 'landed only at the port of Southampton'; any arriving elsewhere were subject to heavy taxation. The arrangement became an Act of Parliament in 1563, in the reign of Queen Elizabeth, the same year in which the town was struck by an outbreak of the plague. The doors of the infected were marked with crosses, and sufferers were made to carry white rods in public to make them known to others. In the autumn, the Corporation engaged twelve of the townspeople (six men and six women) to care for the afflicted and, in many cases, take them to their place of burial. They were paid 1s per week and their employment lasted until the end of the year.

Further bad news was not far behind. The royal attempt to invigorate Southampton's economy incurred the displeasure of the Venetians, who wished to use London. In conjunction with London merchants, they mounted a long and arduous legal battle against the monopoly, costing the Southampton Corporation dearly in expenses. The opposing factions finally agreed to a form of compromise in 1567: wines landed at other ports would still attract heavy taxation, but half of it was to be paid to Southampton as compensation. The Italians were undeterred from using London and paid the duties, which were intended to fund the maintenance and improvement of Southampton's defences. The town's income increased, but trade going through the port did not.

Also in 1567, a group of Protestant refugees settled in Southampton and helped to generate a brief but worthwhile upturn in the town's fortunes. Among the refugees were experienced cloth-makers and merchants, and they soon started to produce serge, the first time that it had been manufactured in England. Customs receipts rose dramatically from 1569 and maintained a healthy level for most of the 1570s, despite a trade embargo with Spain and the Netherlands in the early part of the decade. At around the same time another source of traffic in the port came from a less respectable activity: the Channel swarmed with English privateers in French and Dutch pay, who targeted

Spanish vessels and landed their booty at Southampton. With the resurgent trade with France and Portugal in wines, oil and fruit, the port was thriving once more – at least temporarily.

When the embargo on trade with Spain expired in 1573, business with the Spanish also recovered, but typically of Southampton's fluctuating commercial life, the prosperity was short-lived. In 1577, a collective of merchants based in London formed the Spanish Company and secured a monopoly on trade conducted between England and Spain, removing it from Southampton. The following decade has been described as one of deep depression in the town. Documents of 1582 suggest various additional causes: the wool trade shifted to Lyme, Taunton and Bristol, while canvas markets relocated to Salisbury. Several merchants faced bankruptcy after 'losses at sea', while others simply lacked the wherewithal to run their businesses effectively.

It was also in 1582 that some of the town's more adventurous merchants speculated on the success of Sir Humphrey Gilbert's voyage to North America in an attempt to secure trade routes with Newfoundland. The expedition took place the following year. Not only did it fail to bring the desired economic respite, but the investors never saw their money again. Gilbert's ships successfully landed in Newfoundland, although the voyagers chose not to settle because of a lack of supplies. On the return journey, Gilbert and his ship, *The Squirrel* went down in a storm and with them the financial hopes of a number of Southampton merchants. Also in 1583, to add insult to injury, a further bout of plague swept through the town, leading to a marked increase in recorded burials and, doubtless, many more unrecorded.

Spain had by this time become a dominant world power, and relations with England were fragile. Queen Elizabeth supported the Portuguese in their disputes with Philip II of Spain, who in turn wished to conquer the English and add another territory to his empire. After a period of heightening tension, war broke out in 1585. Three years later, Southampton was ordered to contribute two ships and one small auxiliary vessel to the campaign, as Francis Drake prepared to face the Armada. At this stage, however, the Corporation had ingratiated itself with Secretary of State, Sir Francis Walsingham, who had family connections, both with the locality and the queen. Walsingham appealed on the town's behalf, reasoning that the demand for three ships was excessive for a port in such a sorry condition; eventually just one was provided.

The ship in question was the *Angel*, which served as a fire ship – used to repel the Spanish attackers and drive them back around Scotland, to their eventual doom in treacherous storms. Captain of *Angel* was Lawrence Prowse, an affluent Southampton merchant who would later become mayor.

The greater impact of the war in Southampton was that the privateering that had emerged in the 1570s was no longer illegal: Spanish vessels were targeted (nominally at least) as part of the ongoing war effort. Once more piracy benefited the town's economy, as moneyed London businessmen saw an opportunity to take advantage of the conflict and used Southampton as their base. As the 1590s progressed, the town's industries servicing the privateers flourished: shipbuilders' business naturally increased, ships' crews sought food and accommodation, and some of the hijacked goods were traded before the remainder was returned to London.

By 1596, Southampton's population had risen to over 4,000, but by the end of the century, its economy had dwindled again. The war with Spain had not been as bitterly fought since the death of Philip II in 1598 and the impact on the town was swift: Southampton's customs receipts in 1600 were the lowest for a century. The decline was not just commercial; an air of decay permeated the town. Walls and defences were unkempt and crumbling, overtaken by vegetation rather than attacking forces. Some of the towers were even inhabited by poor people who were unable to afford their own homes; they destroyed defensive features to adapt them to residential use. The castle itself was empty and falling into ruin. Its north wall had been demolished over a century earlier, with the stone being used to build Town Watergate Quay, and, by 1585, the remaining perimeter walls had largely gone as well. Elizabeth stayed at the castle in 1591 (after previous visits in 1560 and 1569), so the keep itself must still have been in reasonable condition, but the building never again served as a defensive structure.

Despite many periods of adversity over the last five centuries, Tudor House in St Michael's Square retains a prominent position in Southampton's architectural and cultural landscape, and another chapter in its long and colourful history has begun. The house has passed through the hands of many owners over the years and, in the middle of the nineteenth century, it was divided into small units, some of which were used as workshops. This period left the building in a somewhat sorry condition, but it was saved from further deterioration when it was purchased by a man named William Spranger in about 1890. To a large extent Spranger was the saviour of Tudor House: as the nineteenth century ended and the twentieth century began he oversaw an extensive restoration programme that attempted to return the building to its appearance of nearly 400 years earlier. With the work complete, Spranger turned philanthropist, and, in 1911, he sold the house to Southampton Corporation for less than the cost of the renovations. The following year, Tudor House was opened as a museum – the first of its kind in Southampton – and has remained as such ever since. By the end of the twentieth century, the ravages of time were once again taking their toll and more work was undertaken to secure the structure of the building. In 2002, the museum was closed to enable a complete refurbishment, jointly funded by a Lottery grant and Southampton City Council. The intricate work took nine years to complete and included the installation of a 15-ton concrete pillar to prevent any further structural subsidence. Boasting a new lift and a café as well as state-of-the-art exhibition technology, Tudor House reopened in 2011. It is set for many more years as a landmark building in Southampton.

Lovingly restored and reopened to the public: Tudor House Museum, 2011.

five

MAYFLOWER, CIVIL WAR & PLAGUE

Despite the abject failure of Sir Humphrey Gilbert's expedition to Newfoundland in 1583, Southampton's merchants and seamen went on to gain valuable experience of Atlantic journeys. Since the port was also well placed geographically for such a voyage, it was chosen as the embarkation point of one of the most famous transatlantic crossings in history. However, fate and the passage of time have meant that the epic journey of the Pilgrim Fathers (or the Forefathers, as they were first known) is now more closely associated with Plymouth.

The ship that made the landmark journey, the *Mayflower*, was a typical merchant vessel – around 100ft long and weighing 180 tons. Her commanding officer, as for the previous eleven years, was Christopher Jones, who also had an ownership stake in the ship. Jones had overseen many Channel crossings in *Mayflower*, primarily taking wool to France and bringing wine back, although transport of other provisions also took the ship to a variety of European ports. In the summer of 1620, *Mayflower* was hired by Thomas Weston, a London businessman who intended to reap a double benefit from moving to America: the opportunity to hasten the advancement of religion and also to make a healthy financial reward.

Mayflower arrived in Southampton from London in late July 1620, already carrying around seventy of the passengers who were hoping to emigrate to the New World. They were joined by additional pilgrims from Holland, fewer than fifty in number, who left Delfshaven on 1 August aboard *Speedwell*; this had been purchased especially for the expedition. A mention in Southampton's 'Book of Instrument' in October 1606 suggests that by visiting Southampton *Speedwell* was in fact returning to her place of construction, since it documents a vessel of the same name and of consistent size and tonnage (she was only a third of the size of *Mayflower* at 60 tons). However, whether they were one and the same, cannot be stated with certainty.

Upon arrival at the port it became obvious that *Speedwell* required maintenance if she was to continue the journey, necessitating a delay of almost a fortnight and expense that the operation's leaders had neither foreseen nor allowed for financially. The enforced hiatus produced a brief boom for the shopkeepers of Southampton, as the emigrants ventured into the town to buy provisions that would sustain them while repairs were undertaken: naturally, the stores on board the two ships were intended for the journey itself, rather than to be frittered away before setting sail. Since Southampton was supposed to be the last port of call before landing in the New World, any other last-minute purchases would also have been made in the town.

During the two-week delay, twenty-year-old John Alden joined the ranks of the emigrants; although it cannot be definitively stated that he was a Southampton man, significant circumstantial evidence suggests it. An Alden family can be traced back to the fifteenth century in the town, by about 1600 occupying a High Street house close to the Bargate. George Alden (possibly John's father) worked as an arrow maker for over thirty years, and last appears in the town records in the summer of 1620. If George died at this time, John may have been left alone and perhaps saw nothing to prevent his embarking on a new life across the Atlantic. Furthermore, Southampton's governors were ordered to pressgang 100 men of John's age, strength and skills in July 1620, and Alden may have considered that becoming a Pilgrim was the preferable option. Speculation aside, John Alden joined the emigrants as a cooper, charged with responsibility for the stores of water, beer and other provisions.

Meanwhile, the lack of progress led to doubts about the success of the whole venture, even at the highest levels. Robert Cushman, one of the expedition leaders, wrote a letter during his time in Southampton in which he observed that 'if we ever make a plantation God works a miracle'. Nonetheless, with the repairs to *Speedwell* finally completed, the two ships departed from Southampton on Saturday, 15 August 1620. However, the delays and frustrations were by no means over. The work done to *Speedwell* had made little improvement to her seaworthiness – she was as 'leaky as a sieve' according to one description – and both she and *Mayflower* were forced to land at Dartmouth for another fortnight-long repair. Both ships set sail again and this time managed to venture 300 miles before *Speedwell*'s inadequacies resurfaced. They returned to Plymouth, where it was decided that only *Mayflower* could be trusted to make the entire crossing. Since not all of *Speedwell*'s emigrants could be accommodated, around twenty

The Pilgrim Fathers (or *Mayflower*) Memorial acknowledges Southampton's part in the colonisation of North America. It was unveiled in 1913.

had to be left behind. After all these trials and tribulations, *Mayflower* finally left Plymouth on Wednesday, 16 September and reached America a little over two months later. Had *Speedwell* not proved so unreliable, the Pilgrim Fathers' place of settlement might have been immortalised using Southampton's name, and remembered as such for the ensuing centuries. Nearly 300 years after the famous voyage, a memorial was erected on Western Esplanade, commemorating Southampton's perpetually unacknowledged place in the story of the colonisation of the New World.

In March 1625, Charles I became king, succeeding his father James I. That summer, London suffered an outbreak of plague, to the extent that Parliament relocated to Oxford to avoid the pestilence. In August and September, the new monarch visited Southampton, reputedly residing at No.17 High Street, and even completed an agreement known as the Treaty of Southampton with representatives of the United Provinces (the Dutch Republic). Despite the honour and prestige that the king's presence bestowed, however, his visit was a financial burden: the town, together with Salisbury, was required to loan £3,000 'for the wants of his household'. Two years later, Charles came to Southampton again. On this occasion the town's hospitality was neither as lavish nor enduring, although Mayor Knowles presented to the king a mysterious 'covered cup', the contents of which were unrecorded. After this intriguing exchange, Charles ate at the home of Sir John Mill and then stayed the night in Titchfield.

If by this time anyone in Southampton felt aggrieved that Plymouth had somewhat usurped the role of their home in the voyage of the *Mayflower*, other western seaports were hardly endearing themselves to the town either. While Exeter and Bristol flourished, the large part of Southampton's trade was conducted with France and the Channel Islands, mostly dealing with wine, vinegar and cloth. There was, however, a small amount of transatlantic business: Southampton ships visited the fisheries of Newfoundland, traded their purchases in Virginia and then stocked up with tobacco (growing in popularity in the early seventeenth century) for the return voyage to England.

Elsewhere in the town, localised industry was exactly that: a collection of small businesses that served Southampton itself and a small area beyond. One of the few exceptions to this was shipbuilding, situated primarily at West Quay. Both this area and Town Quay were noted in 1635 by a Lieutenant Hammond in a travelogue he compiled of his journey around parts of the country. Hammond described the town as 'very strong walled' with 'many towers', but also pointed out the 'old ruinated castle', which James I had sold in 1618 for just over £2,000. The lieutenant seems to have been especially smitten with Southampton, venturing that the High Street 'transcends any other town street in England', and equally enthusiastic about the townspeople: 'fair, neat, beautiful.'

Southampton's governance underwent a significant change in 1640 when Charles I granted the town a new charter. Although at first glance it was not a radical departure from earlier charters – dealing with the role of the mayor, customs rates, the town's courts and so on – there was a particularly important alteration. Charters detailing Southampton's administration had previously bestowed power on the mayor, bailiffs and burgesses. With the passage of time, a greater and greater number of aldermen had their places on the Corporation's governing body, but they lacked the voting powers of the senior members. Since by this point the aldermen outnumbered the bailiffs and burgesses, the integrity of the decision-making process was brought into question, but the small group controlling the town (rightly described by A. Temple Patterson as an oligarchy) was to have its grip loosened. The charter of 1640 used the term 'common council' in relation to Southampton for the first time, and specified the role of the town's aldermen, granting them 'power to make statutes, bye-laws etc.' alongside their colleagues.

Also in 1640, Southampton was involved in a matter of national interest, when the Puritan writer and reactionary William Prynne landed at the port upon his return to England following incarceration at Jersey. Prynne had published his outspoken views in many books and pamphlets, and his writing about the immorality of the theatre (of performers and spectators alike) was thought to contain thinly veiled attacks on King Charles. His views evidently found favour with the people of Southampton, who gave him a warm reception on his return from exile. Their response set the tone for the town's political stance during the English Civil War.

Along with the majority of centres of business or industry, Southampton came down on the Parliamentarian side in the conflict, even if the town's leaders showed some sympathies towards the Royalists. A system was quickly set up to spread the word should the town come under attack: 'the usual guard of burgesses was set in the wards, who had the authority to sound the alarm, and to rouse the inhabitants by beating drums at any threatening of assault.' In November 1642, Parliament voted in favour of a garrison in Southampton and the town acquiesced in December 1642 when Captain Swanley (ironically commanding a warship called *Charles*) sailed up to the town and demanded its surrender. 'An active partisan of the Parliament', Swanley had already been involved in an attack on Carisbrooke Castle, the capture of Calshot Castle and the disabling of Netley Castle, among other skirmishes in the area. He sent a letter to Mayor Peter Seale in which he recognised Southampton as 'a considerable place of merchandise', but with a polite and barely veiled threat that suggested the Corporation declared itself 'obedient to the commands of Parliament and … the Governor of Portsmouth'. A number of letters were exchanged, Swanley presumably waiting patiently in the meantime, and eventually 'a deputation was sent to Portsmouth to declare that the town would henceforth submit to the authority of Parliament'. Thereafter the Parliamentarians controlled all the ports and fortifications on the Southampton estuary, and, indeed, the Solent – an enviable and highly defendable stronghold. The military strength of the town's position turned out to be something of a blessing, as politically it sat on the divide between a staunchly Parliamentarian area to the east and a predominantly Royalist one to the west (there was a

Royalist garrison as close as Romsey). Since the few westerly Parliamentarian ports were isolated on the coast and surrounded by Royalists, ships from Southampton took much-needed supplies to them via the Channel.

The greatest threat to the town came in the winter of 1643/4 when Royalist troops led by Sir Ralph Hopton advanced eastwards into Hampshire as far as Romsey and Redbridge. But Colonel Richard Norton, a local man and friend of Cromwell, managed to recapture Romsey and at the end of March 1644, Hopton was defeated at the Battle of Cheriton near Winchester. The danger passed. As the conflict wore on, however, Southampton people's support for the Parliamentarians, and, more pertinently, the troops stationed in the town, began to be tested. Prisoners and wounded men were a financial burden and on one inglorious occasion, the latter group threatened the very health of the town. After victory at the Battle of Cheriton, the Earl of Essex (commander-in-chief of the Parliamentarian forces) advanced his troops into Cornwall in the tracks of the vanquished Royalists. However, the manoeuvre backfired: Essex and his men were surrounded; and although the earl himself managed to escape by sea, his troops were forced to march back to Southampton. After what must have been a torturous journey through areas mostly sympathetic to the king, 'a crowd of demoralised, starving, ragged and half naked men' arrived in the town in September 1644. Not only did they incur the town with some of the cost of rehabilitation, treatment and re-equipment, but also their diseases infected many of the people who sought to assist them.

When the Civil War ended in 1649, Oliver Cromwell decreed that Southampton's mayor and two of its aldermen were unsuitable to hold their positions, and that other (presumably more malleable) men should be appointed instead. Similarly, Anglican clergymen were removed from the town's churches and replaced by sectarian ministers. One of these, the Presbyterian Nathaniel Robinson, had been in the town for a number of years and had courted controversy by preaching without being an ordained minister.

In June 1650, the condition of the town walls was assessed and repairs were deemed necessary. Governor Murford, tasked with the upkeep of the fortifications nearly seven years earlier, was given a budget of £250 for the work. But the following year Southampton's defences apparently became a low priority: Murford was relieved of his duties and the town garrison was disbanded. In the summer of 1652, the garrison's guardhouse close to the Bargate was demolished, and the firearms and ammunition were removed. This policy soon appeared ill-founded, however. Friction was growing between the English and

Dutch navies, with the latter – the greatest fleet in the world – controlling vast amounts of ocean-going trade.

Southampton's economy suffered dreadfully as a result, despite the strength of the town's shipbuilding. In the winter of 1652, the mayor was ordered to supply 300 seamen, but by February the following year, only twenty-one could be mustered, 'owing to the lack of trade and but few ships arriving'. Moreover, the merchants whose crews did come to the port applied for exemption from the order, to avoid further business losses. On 18 February 1653, the English and Dutch navies finally engaged in the Solent, and after two days of battle, the English emerged victorious. Fifty Dutch ships were impounded, together with 1,500 prisoners, over 1,000 of whom were taken back to Southampton. The town may have avoided a naval attack, but it soon faced a different threat. Despite an appeal from the mayor, which mentioned the disease brought to the town in 1644, the prisoners remained in Southampton; and plague soon broke out again. Tellingly, when the doctor presented his bill the following year its details went unchecked by the Corporation as no one was prepared to go near him.

Cromwell's Commonwealth was brought to an end by the Restoration in 1660, and the coronation of Charles II took place in April 1661, an event celebrated in Southampton and throughout the country. Mayor Edward Downer led a resplendent civic procession through the streets of the town, which were lined with enthusiastic crowds. Arriving at Holy Rood church the mayor and councillors took part in a service in which they gave thanks for the peaceful return of the monarchy. The old order soon returned: the Corporation leader James Capelin lost his place on the council, and the three men previously removed resumed their civic duties. Also restored were the Anglican priests, at the expense of their replacements, such as Nathaniel Robinson. However, the sectarians remained in Southampton to minister to the most diligent members of their congregations, even risking persecution and incarceration. Robinson died 'at an advanced age' in 1696.

⁓⁓ ⁓⁓

The pestilences brought to Southampton in 1644 and 1653 were soon to appear insignificant. In the summer of 1665, plague broke out in the town, brought (in the opinion of one observer) by an infected child who arrived from London on 6 June. The infant was taken in by a widow and her family, but the disease quickly spread and the entire household perished. By the middle of the month, any house thought to contain the plague was boarded up, and, by 27 June, the total had grown to eight houses. The following day, with the town 'panic stricken', the Corporation was forced to offer incentives to anyone who would take on the risk of disposing of the corpses. Since gravediggers baulked at the thought of dealing with plague victims, a volunteer who agreed to the task was rewarded with the next available place in the guild of town porters – a desirable and profitable position.

In early July, the mayor, Thomas Cornelius, and the few members of the Council still willing and able to undertake the administration of the town, met to discuss the situation. They composed a letter to Lord Ashley, Lord President of the Privy Council, in which they appealed for 'means to prevent that which we have too just a cause to dread, even the utter ruin and desolation of this place and people'. Another document written the next day revealed that the plague was causing the more affluent to flee the town and deterring rural traders from entering it, leading to shortages of supplies.

A reply to the appeal for aid came a week later and expressed King Charles II's sympathies at 'the sad condition' of Southampton: houses lay empty and the streets were becoming overgrown with weeds and grass. Supplies were to be sent from other towns, and the king offered to pay for a doctor. Meanwhile, Mayor Cornelius and his remaining crisis-hardened colleagues set about imposing fines on Corporation members and Church officers who had been so eager to flee both the plague and their duties – a shrewd policy that punished civic desertion and raised valuable funds at the same time. The heaviest fine of £20 was directed at John Steptoe (the deputy mayor and mayor the previous year), 'for neglecting to give his assistance in this time of affliction'. Similar accusations, but lesser financial punishments, were levelled at the town steward and chief bailiff, as well as several of the town's parish churchwardens.

Although the fines were sizeable to those affected, they made little impact on Southampton's costs in managing the epidemic. In the middle of July, the mayor issued a further appeal, directed at all justices of the peace and any other 'charitable persons' in the county, estimating the weekly shortfall at £150. To make matters worse, the continuing spread of the disease was depleting the existing help: 'many of those who lately contributed towards the relief of others are now reduced to that necessity as to need relief themselves.'

The appeals, however, brought better news. The king himself donated £50, while Sarum, where he was staying at the time, gave £70. The Earl of Southampton, fulfilling the role of lord treasurer, also gave £50, and similar contributions came from Dorchester, Portsmouth, Marlborough and Exeter.

Many other towns in southern England sent financial aid (even those as small as Titchfield and Hamble), as did the bishops of Winchester and Norwich. In addition to his £50 donation Charles II also sent twenty tuns of French wine, which were sold to raise further funds after the first half-tun was given to the poor. The sale produced over £240, entirely from Mayor Cornelius and two of his colleagues. Cornelius, as canny as he had been in fining the town's deserters, was thus contributing to the relief fund and simultaneously taking advantage of a good business deal. The historian A. Temple Patterson wryly suggested that in light of the conditions in the town the three councillors possibly used at least a small amount of the wine 'to sustain their own courage with some of the Dutch variety'.

The severity of the pestilence diminished briefly, but, by autumn, it was worsening again; in turn, the preventative measures became more drastic. Once the disease was detected in a household, the building was closed up, with no one allowed to leave, and it was placed under observation should anyone attempt an escape. These precautions, while necessary, inevitably led to heart-wrenching situations. In October 1665, a woman, who had fled to Cowes, paid two sailors to visit Southampton and return with her daughter, who was the last surviving inhabitant in one of the closed-up houses. The two men successfully extricated the girl, but were subsequently apprehended; one of the sailors and the girl were confined, while the other sailor was court-martialled. At the end of the year, it was recorded that around 800 inhabitants of Southampton had perished, but the plague had by then subsided to the extent that people were able to return to their homes. The disease returned in the New Year, far less aggressively, and by the end of 1666 had all but disappeared. However, the town was reminded of the crisis long after the last plague victim had died: in late 1670, a man's belongings, untouched since his death four years earlier, were retrieved from his room and buried. A later estimate of Southampton's death toll from the plague put the figure at 1,700, perhaps over half the town's population.

After the trials of the Civil War and the devastation of the plague, there was still more hardship to come before Southampton saw an upturn in its fortunes. Serge making, the town's only significant manufacturing industry, was gravely affected by the plague, and was dealt a further blow by the Restoration. The mostly dour, parochial clothing of the Commonwealth was cast aside and replaced with more vibrant and colourful fashions, which reflected the rebirth of the nation. Suddenly the serge clothing that had been worn by women of high social standing was considered unfit even for their servants.

Demand for resplendent new outfits was initially met with imports from France until an Act of Parliament curtailed the trade in 1678. This measure, intended to boost the native manufacture of cloth, merely shifted the source of imports from France to India, and the supply of fine foreign fabrics continued. Once again, Southampton's industry began to look inwards, with craftsmen and traders largely reliant on business in the town and nearby countryside.

By 1683, the overseas wine trade had reached a desperate position as well. Duties on sweet wines, which had previously brought £200 a year into the town's coffers, fell to around £6. At the same time, however, shipping between Southampton and other British ports was cause for mild optimism. In 1683, the town was the fourth largest British importer of Newcastle coal, also welcoming fish from Cornwall and Devon and a range of supplies from London and Bristol. Outgoing cargoes to the rest of the country also increased healthily, and, by 1687, the number of shipments leaving Southampton was over half that leaving London.

Alongside this was the revitalised shipbuilding industry, which had improved before the Civil War and remained strong during the life of the Commonwealth, when a number of warships were built in Southampton. Construction died down following the Restoration, but with the outbreak of yet another conflict with France (the War of the League of Augsburg in 1689), the Admiralty placed orders in the town once again. Most such contracts were undertaken at Portsmouth, but the overflow led to the creation of new shipbuilding sites on the western bank of the Itchen at Chapel and Northam.

However, the cautious improvement in the town's prosperity was yet to be reflected in its appearance, which still bore the signs of decline. Edmund Gibson, later Bishop of London, noted that the grand merchants' houses, so symbolic of Southampton's bygone days of healthy overseas commerce, were falling into disrepair and ruin. Furthermore, the resurgence in shipbuilding turned out to be brief, as demand fell away in 1698 when peace with France was restored. In 1696, the town was visited by the extraordinary Celia Fiennes, who travelled the country for many years, passing through every county and keeping a diary of her journeys and thoughts. She described 'a very neat clean town and the streets well pitched and kept', but observed that 'the trade has failed and the town almost forsooke and neglected'. Fiennes, like several others, also noticed the ruined castle and dilapidated fortifications – metaphors, perhaps, for Southampton itself. As the seventeenth century drew to a close the town was by no means forgotten, but certainly forlorn.

AN APPEAL FROM
THE SOUTHAMPTON CORPORATION, JULY 1665

'We cannot believe but that you are acquainted with the very sad and calamitous condition of our poor distressed town by reason of that malignant and pestilential disease which is broken in upon us, and still is raging, putting an utter period to our traffic, driving the richer sort out of the town, and affrighting the country from bring in their accustomed provisions, insomuch as we seem to be threatened with famine as well as pestilence, unless some provident course be taken; and not only so, but it is also much to be feared (if it please not God in some short time to withhold His afflicting hand) that the poorer sort of people wanting relief, and not finding it (there being very few persons of any ability remaining in the town), will be very hardly restrained from breaking forth and wandering abroad to the great danger of infecting the whole neighbourhood.'

six

SPA TOWN

The dawn of the eighteenth century found Southampton in a condition far from its best. The ruined castle continued to crumble and deteriorate, although the keep and bailey walls were still easily recognisable, and parts of the grounds had been used for building houses. The town walls were also in a poor state of repair, and were a financial burden that the Corporation did not consider a high priority. A population of around 3,000 was still mostly contained within these walls, beyond which some additional houses lined the roads leading north from the Bargate and east from the East Gate. Otherwise there were small pockets of civilisation at Portswood and attached to the shipbuilding areas of Chapel and Northam.

As far as Southampton's churches were concerned, the most prominent (and central) was Holy Rood, situated on the High Street halfway between the Bargate and Town Quay. Facing the church was the Audit House, the town's seat of local government along with the Bargate. Members of the Corporation, therefore, attended services at Holy Rood, particularly at times of local or national significance, and the church was used to make important public announcements. Meanwhile, the French church in Winkle Street aligned itself with the Anglican Church in 1712, although the elders and trustees retained control of their property and charities. Some members of the congregation objected to the alliance and formed their own independent French church, but this had disappeared well before the end of the century.

Such a level of diligence and loyalty, however, was not always shared by the Corporation members in undertaking their civic duties. At a number of meetings around this time, there was little or no official business to deal with, and before long attendances dwindled. One day in June 1713, Mayor Gardiner waited in the Audit House for two long hours without being joined by a single one of his colleagues. Predictably, far greater enthusiasm was reserved for celebrated anniversaries (such as that of Charles II's Restoration on 29 May), when the Audit House hosted enormously indulgent feasts. The accession of Queen Anne in March 1702, for example, had been toasted with seventy-two bottles of wine and 'other conveniences as Mr Mayor should think fit'. The banquets accompanying the election of each new mayor were equally opulent, and served to demonstrate the huge gulf between the town's leaders and its citizens.

By the mid-1720s, there were few indications of Southampton's economic rebirth. Daniel Defoe visited and found it 'in a manner dying with age; the decay of the trade is the real decay of the town'. With the French wine trade at a low-ebb and much of the Newfoundland fishing trade relocating to Poole, things looked bleak. There may indeed have been 'much smuggling', as Defoe observed, but this of course contributed nothing to the town's taxation revenue or reputa-

Winkle Street, close to God's House Tower, as photographed in 1890 but largely unchanged for many years.

tion. However, if Southampton's finances were less than healthy, at least the town's cultural aspect was looking up, as it was around this time that Charles Mordaunt, Earl of Peterborough, purchased the Bevois Mount estate north of the town walls.

Mordaunt had led an eventful life, having served as First Lord of the Treasury, being imprisoned in the Tower of London, and then leading English troops in Spain so erratically that he was charged with incompetence upon his return. He was friendly with a number of prominent literary figures and welcomed to his home such luminaries as Voltaire, Jonathan Swift and Alexander Pope, who was said to be particularly smitten with the area. The estate was described in some detail in 1743, by Jeremiah Miles, after Mordaunt's death. Miles had little time for Mordaunt's aesthetic preferences as far as his buildings were concerned, but was more enthusiastic about the gardens, which included a summer house with views across the town to the Isle of Wight. The original farmhouse had been rebuilt in the style of a Corinthian temple – 'in a tolerable good taste' – and was further adapted and enhanced by Mordaunt's widow. The prevailing problem with the estate, according to Miles, was that when the tide was out in the River Itchen (which was most of the day), 'the slobby channel appearing takes greatly from the beauty of the prospect'. During his life, Mordaunt was said only to be willing to welcome visitors when the tide was in and the view more pleasing.

Still struggling financially, meanwhile, Southampton Corporation began to be somewhat flexible with its morals in order to generate additional income. In a practice far from uncommon in parliamentary boroughs around the country at the time, nomination as a member of parliament could essentially be purchased – if the candidate and price were right. Sometimes the 'generous' candidate faced no competition at all, but even when he did the Corporation possessed enough influence and ingenuity to ensure that the results of the election were not in doubt. The policy brought significant and invaluable revenue to the town – £200 in 1722 and 700 guineas in 1728. With these sizeable injections of cash, Southampton's finances improved considerably.

At about the same time, a new fashion was developing that would enhance the prosperity of the town on a grand scale. Spa water was becoming popular to a hitherto unprecedented level, with its perceived medicinal qualities finding increasing favour. A number of existing spa towns already enjoyed the economic benefits brought about by the arrival of health-conscious visitors, and other towns blessed with mineral springs began to see the commercial opportunities. For example, Tunbridge Wells had been known for its waters since the middle of the previous century, while springs had been discovered at Cheltenham in 1716. One of Southampton's springs was at Houndwell, providing water that was 'good for the eyes', according to testimony. Later there was also 'the chalybeate water to the west of the Bargate', which purportedly became 'famous for numberless remarkable cures'.

The town also found itself able to accommodate the other simultaneously growing fashion of sea bathing. Salt water was said to be a particularly good remedy for those bitten by a mad dog, and many came to Southampton's waterside with this specific complaint, sometimes even bringing their infected pets for treatment too. However, the prospects of maximising this aspect were limited as the town's shores lacked picturesque and welcoming beaches: those stretches of seafront not given over to shipping quays were largely unattractive and muddy. To compensate, a number of baths were built so that potential bathing custom would not be lost, including Martin's and Simcox's baths – 'commodious for people of fashion'.

Southampton's acclaim as a stylish spa resort was greatly enhanced by a visit in 1750 from the Prince of Wales – George II's son Frederick. The prince died the following year aged only forty-four, but his three sons, the dukes of York, Gloucester and Cumberland, went on to continue the family's patronage. Such royal endorsement led to the peak of Southampton's spa popularity, and affluent Londoners often visited the town, taking the waters by day and attending lavish masked balls in the evenings. Author, historian and politician, Horace Walpole, wrote of his trip to Southampton in 1755, describing crowded streets and evening walks along the seafront. The vacations were not always idyllic, however: the luxuries afforded to the visiting upper classes created discord among the less opulent locals and sometimes led to physical attacks on wealthy tourists. Nevertheless, the visitors were undeterred and, in 1756, James Hanway recorded that, 'great numbers of people of distinction prefer Southampton for bathing'. While its reputation never matched that of Bath, it was considered the equal of most other spa towns. In fact, Southampton was fortunate to have the spa fashion to compensate for its other economic shortcomings. Richard Pococke noted in 1757 that 'there is but little trade at this town, and if it had not of late been much frequented for bathing and drinking the salt waters they would have had very little commerce, except among themselves'.

The increasing popularity created demand for new buildings in which its visitors could be entertained. In 1761, John Martin built a room from which the more reserved observers could watch adventurous bathers, presumably with feelings of fascinated intrigue and perhaps admiration. Six years later, Martin renovated the premises and they developed into one of the town's most prominent social venues, imaginatively christened the Long Rooms. Located on the south-western coast of the Southampton peninsula, with the water on one side and the arcaded section of the ancient town walls on the other, the premises were 'fitted up at vast expense, in a most elegant manner'. The Long Rooms hosted balls two or three nights a week, between May and October, with an additional special ball every Saturday. Proceedings began at around 7 p.m. and finished at 11 p.m. sharp, even if a dance was still in progress. The code of etiquette stated that gentlemen were prohibited from dancing while wearing boots and (sensibly) carrying swords. Ladies, meanwhile, were not permitted to dance while wearing 'an apron, mittens or black gloves'. In later years, a winter season was also introduced, with fortnightly assemblies held on Tuesday nights at the Dolphin Hotel in the High Street.

The Long Rooms, adjacent to the ancient town walls, was the centre of Southampton's social scene as spa water and bathing became fashionable in the mid-eighteenth century.

Throughout the year, the festivities were overseen by a master of ceremonies, described as 'an official hardly second in importance to the mayor himself'. The man appointed to the role was essentially all-powerful within the confines of the social events and was doubtless a figure of great esteem without them. The master of ceremonies introduced newcomers at functions, after approving their suitability, and ensured that rules were strictly observed in line with the printed copies available for reference. Periodic appointments of a new master of ceremonies were seen as vitally important, and the elite turned out in great numbers. For the election of a Mr Haynes, in January 1786, for example, the meeting held was described as the 'fullest and most respectable ever seen upon almost any occasion'. Haynes, however, was only to have two successors before the role became obsolete.

Elsewhere, a further evening diversion could be found at the new theatre in French Street, close to the site of a previous theatre. Daytime recreation was provided by the libraries and coffee houses that were opening at this time. London and regional newspapers were available in these establishments, and groups of socialites met to discuss and digest the news of the day. One of these newspapers, the *Hampshire Chronicle*, was originated and first published in the town, but later relocated to Winchester. Southampton was soon benefiting from several coach services that connected the town with popular destinations, including London, Oxford and Bristol. Competing coach companies sought to outdo one another with their advertisements in the local press, slashing their fares and in some cases literally racing alongside each other in order to boast that they offered the fastest service. Higher speeds naturally brought increased risks and accidents were by no means unusual, with both passengers and pedestrians injured.

Considerably safer perambulations, meanwhile, were available along a popular walk known as the Beach, the waterfront to the east of God's House Tower. The area was renovated and attractively planted, and many visitors to the town strolled and socialised there. Southampton's rapidly growing reputation was reflected in an entry in Baker's *Guide Book*: 'There is no neighbourhood in Britain exclusively of the nobility and gentry who annually honour it with their presence during the summer season, where politeness, harmony and friendship reign so universally.' In 1768, the Duke of York died, but his brothers graced Southampton with their visits for another ten years.

Indeed, at this time Southampton could perhaps have eclipsed its rivals (excepting Bath) if plans for a grand series of buildings outside the town walls

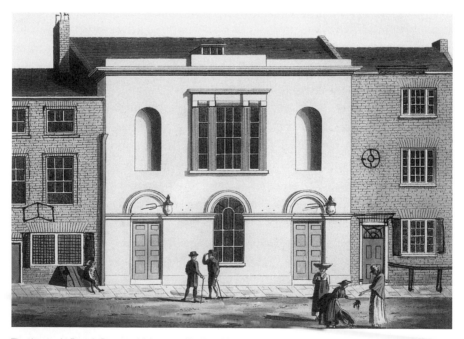

The theatre in French Street, which opened in the mid-1760s, was an indicator of the town's prosperity in its days as a popular spa resort.

had reached successful fruition. The Long Rooms were, naturally, sited with a view to convenience for the waters. Access to social occasions was difficult in a horse-drawn carriage and a journey on foot increased the chance of an unpleasant encounter with an unwelcoming local. Perhaps just as offensive to the noblest partygoers was the need to share the venue with 'lowly' tradesmen, who also attended the functions. Therefore, it was decided to erect new buildings in place of the Long Rooms, an architectural formation that would rival the finest areas of Bath itself, particularly the Royal Crescent (under construction at the time), and have an appropriate air of exclusivity. Primary funding for this enterprise came from General John Carnac and local property owner, Isaac Mallortie. Carnac had made his fortune from a career in the army of the East India Company, and had returned to Britain from India in 1767. He shared his journey back to Britain with imperial despot Robert Clive, who succeeded Carnac as commander-in-chief of India. Carnac became the MP for Leominster in Herefordshire in 1768, and, despite having difficulties transferring his money back to England, he was comfortably off enough to proceed with the Southampton scheme.

The site for the grand endeavour was to the north-west of the Marlands, less than a mile from the walled town. Stretching to over 20 acres, the location boasted 'a most delightful prospect of Southampton Water as far as Calshot Castle, with fine views of the New Forest'. The architect chosen was Jacob Leroux, a London man already known to Carnac from working on alterations to his Cams Hall mansion near Fareham. Leroux had also designed a number of houses in London, including a large extension to Carlisle House in Soho Square. Pertinently, Carlisle House had become a key venue in London's social scene in the 1760s, attracting the attention of Southampton visitor Horace Walpole. Leroux's idea for the new south-coast scheme was a circle of twelve grand houses surrounding an inner section, which would contain a hotel and shops. This polygon design would give the project, and subsequently the area, its name. The foundation stone of the hotel was laid in August 1768 by the Southampton's two MPs, Henry Viscount Palmerston and Hans Stanley. (The latter, a former peace-broker in negotiations with France over the Seven Years War, met a grisly end in 1780, when he took his own life by cutting his throat.)

By August 1771, the hotel was all but complete, although only two of the shops (a jewellers' and a hairdresser's) were occupied. The scene was recorded by a number of observers, one of whom described 'a most magnificent hotel, in which there is a fine ballroom, card, tea and two billiard rooms, several eating

The ill-fated Polygon scheme, begun in 1768, never fulfilled its ambition or promise of rivalling the Royal Crescent in Bath.

rooms, and they say fifty good bedchambers and stabling for five hundred horses ... I never saw so great a preparation for luxury and elegance.' The hotel was already hosting a ball once a week, but there was some reticence among revellers to make the additional journey from the town, so the hotelier, Mr Frère, provided coaches.

Work soon began on the houses encircling the hotel. Elsewhere in Southampton, other building projects were also under way. The Audit House, Southampton's seat of local government along with the Bargate, had sat in the middle of the High Street since the early part of the fourteenth century – the lower floor accommodating market traders. Over the years, the town's poultry and fish markets had been incorporated into the building, and, in 1763, major renovations had been made to the whole premises, but, in 1771, the Council decreed that the antiquated edifice should be replaced altogether. A new and more convenient site previously owned by one of the town's aldermen was acquired, opposite the Red Lion public house. The London architect, John Crunden, was contacted at his Piccadilly residence and he agreed to take on the scheme. Crunden was best known at the time as an author and compiler of pattern books – essentially collections of standardised architectural designs that builders could purchase and use. His own preference was for a Classical Palladian style and his designs were popular for many years to come. As an architect in his own right, Crunden completed only a small number of buildings.

One was Portswood House, a second Southampton project, also constructed in 1771. On 27 September, the foundation stone of the new Audit House was laid and it was opened just over two years later, on 5 October 1773. The result was a compact but impressive building featuring a Portland stone façade with richly decorated Ionic columns. The upper floor comprised the council chamber, mayor's parlour, committee rooms and the town clerk's and medical officer's rooms, and storage for the town's valuable archives. On the front of the Audit House was a small wrought-iron balcony overlooking the High Street, from which civic officials could make public announcements. The lower floor, which occupied the entire space between the High Street and French Street, was again given over to accommodation for most of the town's markets, although traders initially disliked their new home.

The Polygon scheme, meanwhile, was not developing as quickly as its promoters might have hoped. In 1772, Leroux revealed his plans for more shops and a chapel, but these additions were never to materialise. By 1773, only three of the houses encircling the hotel had been completed and two of them were occupied by Carnac and Mallortie. More encouragingly, the hotel itself was already the centre of the town's social scene, but even the continued patronage of the dukes of Cumberland and Gloucester could not imbue the Polygon with enough prestige to ensure its completion. Carnac's finances faltered and he was forced to return to India. The hotel faced increasing competition from others within the town walls, particularly the Dolphin. This was rebuilt in 1775, having originally consisted of two properties joined together.

When the Polygon Hotel was put up for sale it attracted so little interest that it was eventually demolished. Some of the land was sold, but the scheme enjoyed a brief final flourish when three more of the proposed houses came to fruition. One of these was later turned into a hotel and was redeveloped in the 1930s, and Handel Terrace now approximates part of the original carriage drive encircling the site. The failure of the Polygon scheme probably achieved more notoriety than anything else, but the area subsequently became a desirable suburb, especially as the town continued to grow northwards. Jacob Leroux, however, did not abandon his concept, and designed another scheme called the Polygon in Somers Town, London: this time consisting of thirty-two houses. Work began in 1791, but was again plagued by financial difficulties and was unfinished at the time of his death in 1799.

With the Polygon fulfilling neither its potential nor its aspirations, John Martin's Long Rooms re-emerged as Southampton's prominent social venue.

The huge value of Martin's contribution to the town's social scene (and thus its economy) is reflected in the fact that his application to demolish parts of the town walls was favourably looked upon by the Corporation. In April 1775, Martin was granted permission 'to take down parts of three round towers on the West Quay', and in June his wish to remove part of a wall over the Biddlesgate was also approved. The towers and wall were close to the ancient arcade, near enough to the Long Rooms that their removal apparently enhanced both the appearance of the area and its safety for the benefit of Martin's customers.

Today the reckless destruction of medieval architecture may seem ill-advised, but the notion of preservation and heritage is a relatively modern one, and the choice was made purely with reference to the town's economy and social standing. As Davies observed, 'the Corporation did not hesitate when it became a question of whether Mr Martin or the towers should go'. Initially at least the Council's decision appeared to have the desired effect, as both the town and the Long Rooms maintained their popularity with visitors. 'In the summer Southampton is much resorted to by people of fashion, who bathe in the sea and drink the salt water,' wrote John Swete, in 1777, going on to praise the quality of the seafood and port available in the town.

Elsewhere in Southampton, other improvements were helping to make the town a better place for both residents and visitors. In 1770, the Corporation had obtained an Act of Parliament relating to the town's paving, public lighting and policing. Paving had fallen under the Council's authority since 1749, but a large part of the responsibility was placed upon householders, who had to maintain the pavement and road directly outside their homes. The policy was less than effective and street conditions deteriorated: the High Street was only passable for carriages on one side, and other roads were potholed and dirty. Under the 1770 Act, a number of paving commissioners were appointed, and this signalled the moment at which the Council began to take responsibility both for the appearance of the town and to some extent for the welfare of the people who used the roads and pavements. The commissioners, however, only had authority for primary thoroughfares: small side streets and alleyways remained untended 'dumping grounds for every sort of filth'.

The commissioners at least ensured that the most used streets – those primarily seen by visitors – were improved, and thus provided more comfortable journeys for those in carriages. As 1775 drew to a close, the commissioners' work was well under way, if only to the extent that their jurisdiction allowed. Obstacles had been removed from pavements and new street signs installed, while buildings were being properly numbered. Perilous (but commonplace) actions such as leaving cellar doors open became prosecutable offences, and carriages that were left to block streets were removed and chained to a tree until they were reclaimed by their owners. This tree was soon christened Pound Tree and its approximate location was later acknowledged in the naming of Pound Tree Road. Enforcement of these prohibitions to some extent brought into play the policing aspects of the 1770 Act, but public lighting was barely addressed until the early 1780s, when 150 lamps were purchased and installed in the main streets and the dankest areas of the side streets. These lamps were lit in the evenings between September and March, a luxury for which, naturally, the townspeople faced an increase in rates.

The policing of the town still left much to be desired. A night watch existed briefly, but, in its absence, there was little to reassure the citizens. Even Mayor Arthur Atherley was a target for crime in October 1784 when he was attacked and robbed by a highwayman while crossing the Common on his way home one afternoon. Somewhat ironically, the incident took place a mere stone's throw from the town gallows, situated near what is now the junction of The Avenue and Burgess Road. The gallows were used for the last time the following summer in the case of the former servant of a Mrs Bagenal, who had broken into and burgled her Above Bar home. He was tried and found guilty at the Bargate on 9 July 1785, and was hanged later that month.

The public had little faith in the town's policing and before long some of them took matters into their own hands. A privately organised body called the Society of Guardians for the Protection of Property and Persons was created in 1788, and sought to assist its members by publicising crimes perpetrated against them. This was done by taking out advertisements in the local press; where possible, these offered descriptions of the criminals. Witnesses and informants were encouraged to provide evidence with the incentive of financial reward, and once a suspect was identified, the society paid the cost of arrest and prosecution.

By the end of 1788, however, the Corporation was no longer able to cope without a properly ordered and official police force. On Bonfire Night that November, Southampton was the scene of an infamous riot, which arose from a prohibition forbidding the lighting of fires in the streets. Substantial crowds chose to ignore the edict and took exception to its attempted enforcement by the town's meagre representation of justice officers. Both they and the mayor were subjected to a torrid evening, and the paving commissioners were finally convinced to appoint the eight nightwatchmen legally allowed. Whether through fear of taking on the role or simple lack of interest, applicants failed to reach even this number, and only four watchmen were actually appointed, with one other in a supervisory capacity. Their headquarters were at the Bargate, from where the head watchman dispatched his staff after supplying them with necessary equipment for their duties. The four watchmen were each given regular beats to patrol in search of unruly persons; such a transgressor faced a residency in the Bargate jail until being brought before a magistrate for assessment. These measures may have helped the people of Southampton feel more safe and secure, but the coming years brought a potentially far greater threat to their wellbeing.

In the early part of the eighteenth century, one of Southampton's famous sons was coming to prominence. Isaac Watts was born in French Street in Southampton, in 1674. His father (also Isaac) was a man of strongly independent religious convictions, who, in the year of his son's birth, was 'imprisoned in the town gaol for nonconformity'. In 1688, Watts senior became a founding member of the Above Bar church, and in time, all of his children were baptised there. Isaac the younger attended King Edward VI School, where he learnt the Classical languages, then trained for four years at Stoke Newington under the tutelage of Thomas Rowe, a renowned Dissenter. He returned to Southampton in 1694 and soon remarked that he considered the standard of hymns prevailing in churches at the time to be inadequate. In response, his father challenged him to compose something of greater quality, and so began a journey that would come to an end over 600 hymns later. Watts's first collection, *Hymns and Spiritual Songs*, was published in 1707.

Isaac left Southampton for London again in 1696, but visited the town of his birth a number of times over the years. In his later life, he devoted much of his time to writing on religious and philosophical matters, completing works such as *The Improvement of the Mind* and *The Freedom of the Human Will*. However, after his death in November 1748 it was his hymns for which he was best remembered, and many of them are still in regular use today. They include 'There Is a Land of Pure Delight' and 'When I Survey the Wond'rous Cross'. In Southampton, Watts is commemorated by a statue in the city's West Park (often known as Watts Park) and by the Memorial United Reformed church on Winchester Road, which bears his name. Most of all, however, it is the hymn 'O God Our Help In Ages Past' which holds the closest connection to Watts's place of birth: its tune is played by the chimes of the Civic Centre clock tower four times a day, and it is the school hymn of King Edward VI School. It is regularly sung at the city's Armistice Day services and is often known simply as 'Southampton's hymn'.

Isaac Watts's statue in West Park, 2011.

seven

MILITARY MIGHT

outhampton's heyday as a fashionable spa resort finally led to improvements in the town's commercial prosperity. New shops were opened in the main streets, some of them by London retailers: if their clientele spent summer on the south coast, they would too. Southampton was soon home to a number of high-class suppliers of hats, hosiery, dresses and linen, all in the latest styles and frequently restocked with new deliveries from the capital.

By the late 1780s, the town's port trade was healthier, estimated to be a fifth higher than only ten years before. Commerce with the rest of Britain fell away slightly, but this was more than compensated for by the expansion of business with the Channel Islands. Further afield there was lively trade with Ireland, northern Germany and the Baltic countries, and packet boats regularly crossed back and forth to Le Havre. The consequence of the economic upturn was that the town's wharves and quays soon became incapable of handling the increased traffic. Moreover, merchants were frustrated with the self-serving policies of the Corporation, and began to challenge the status quo.

The dispute centred on the ownership of the quaysides – the Corporation was unable to provide enough accommodation to meet demand and yet still insisted on collecting duties on goods landed at privately owned wharves. Aaron Moody had built his own wharf close to his home in the Chapel area and objected to being taxed, as he saw it, for the use of his personal property. A meeting was held at which a group of merchants agreed to challenge the Corporation's 'claim to petty customs' at such private wharves and quays, and Moody offered the use of his wharf to anyone who joined him in refusing to pay the duties. Predictably, the Corporation countered with legal action against a number of the merchants. In instances involving quays owned by the town (such as that against Thomas Baker, an importer of a variety of goods from the Baltic) the Corporation's demands for payment were upheld; but Aaron Moody secured a landmark victory, and the Corporation quickly withdrew its claims in other similar cases.

To compound matters further, the town's governing body soon came under attack on other fronts as well. It was suggested that the councillors should either be replaced en masse or that the Corporation should essentially be dissolved and the administration of the town included with that of the county as a whole. In late 1788, the Corporation set about preserving its status by bolstering its ranks with new members taken from the town's wealthier echelons. 'Those of superior rank' were cordially invited to join the cause, to keep 'the inferior class of inhabitants' at bay, being as they were 'immersed in such complicated wickedness'. The plea was a swift success. Thirteen gentlemen put themselves forward, and they were elected as burgesses on 3 November, along with a further eight shortly afterwards. In the last decade of the century these new members virtually monopolised Southampton's key positions of power (mayor and sheriff), and control of the town was firmly back in the hands of the select few.

The Corporation continued to come under fire, however, when more disagreements over customs charges led to questions about the town's income and expenditure. A campaign asking the Corporation to publish its full accounts was fiercely waged, with the publication of many pamphlets and many letters in the local press. True to form, the Corporation vehemently held its ground, and the issue remained without firm resolution until it was overtaken in importance by matters of national as well as local significance. The French Revolution in 1789 had created an anxiety in neighbouring Europe that radicalism would spread beyond its country of origin. In the prevailing atmosphere, loyalty to the Crown and moral fortitude took on extra importance, and fortuitously for the town's aldermen and councillors attacks on bodies of authority in general were diffused.

When George III recovered from illness, in March 1789, a special ball was held at the Long Rooms, attended by 'all the nobility and gentry of the town and neighbourhood'. The 250 guests danced until midnight and then entered the supper room to the accompaniment of the national anthem. Southampton further displayed its royal allegiance in June of the same year when the king, Queen Charlotte and many members of their household visited the town while staying at Lyndhurst. Corporation members received the royal party at the Audit House, and the king and queen later toured the seafront, 'expressing their delight' at the picturesque views on offer. It therefore came as little surprise that when George made a proclamation against seditious literature in the summer of 1792 the Corporation was quick to send him a statement of loyalty, and an assurance that the town had not been blighted by any 'inflammatory papers' or 'pernicious doctrines' indicative of revolutionary zeal. Within two years, the British government was attempting to prosecute purveyors of such literature with charges tantamount to treason, although a backlash over the loss of civil liberties ensued.

In December 1792, the Corporation added its support to a declaration made by the City of London promising to uphold the constitution 'in the present state of affairs'. At an Audit House meeting of the townspeople – thought at the time to be the largest of its kind held – the engagingly titled Association for Preserving Liberty and Property against the Machinations of Republicans and Levellers, and for the Support of our Happy Constitution was created. Also known, presumably for the sake of brevity, as the Loyal Association, the body soon received an assurance from the town's publicans that they would attempt to monitor any plotting in their premises and inform the authorities accordingly. When the war with France did indeed begin, in early 1793, the town sent yet another address of loyalty to the king.

For neither the first nor the last time in its history, Southampton quickly took on the appearance of a town at war. In June 1795, a force of 4,000 men left from the port, taking arms for five times greater than their number. Arriving by sea in August that year John Manners recorded: 'Nothing can equal the beauty of the shores on each side, going up Southampton Water. Numbers of beautiful villas, surrounded by woods, appeared on all sides.' But upon landing a different picture presented itself: 'As soon as we got into the town, nothing but red coats and military were to be seen.' A large camp for the troops was located outside Southampton at Nursling Common under the supervision of Lord Moira, who was no stranger to the town; the previous year his men had also camped there, and left from Southampton bound for France. Movements in and out of the camp were frequent. Manners noted that six regiments had recently departed, for a destination unknown to those they left behind, while another had just returned from Jersey, having lost 250 men to an outbreak of fever. Also present was the 42nd Highland Regiment, otherwise known as the Black Watch, 'which is reckoned to be the best in service'.

The presence of additional people in and around Southampton helped to enhance the upturn in economic prosperity begun by the fashion for spa water earlier in the century. Extra men created a need for food and clothing at the very least, while the more senior officers patronised the town's taverns and hosted social functions to rival the existing balls. Therefore, benefits extended to the shopkeepers, merchants and small industrialists of Southampton, all of whom saw an increase in demand for their goods and services. Furthermore, all the expenditure consisted of money originating outside the town: the practice at the time was for regiments to be posted to areas away from their homes in order to obviate any temptations to return to domestic comforts if there was the opportunity. The men of Southampton thus found themselves carrying out their garrison duties in Kent, with troops from other counties taking their place. These regiments often received visits from friends and relatives during their service, which, while making something of a mockery of the deployment policy, compensated for the loss of other visitors during hostilities.

In the meantime, shipbuilding in the yards of Southampton and the surrounding areas had experienced something of a renaissance, hastened inevitably by the advent of war with Holland in 1780 and later with France. After a quiet first part of the century the town's shipbuilders had been increasingly occupied in the 1740s and again, after a further lull, in the 1770s and 1780s. Even greater activity, however, was to be seen in the yards at Bursledon and Bucklers Hard, to the east and west of Southampton Water respectively. Although, like Southampton, neither yard was busy in the 1760s, they were otherwise prodigious in their output. Bucklers Hard in particular was a significant supplier of vessels that would have roles to play in the conflict, many of them built under the direction of Henry Adams who lived and worked in the village for over sixty years. Of these, probably the most famous was the *Agamemnon*, launched in April 1781 and twelve years later, commanded by Horatio Nelson. In fact, Nelson seemed to hold a special affection for the ship, and despite her hard-fought years of service, he later included her in his fleet at Trafalgar.

By early 1796, barracks were being built and equipped in Southampton and its neighbouring districts, some three years after the town's publicans had appealed for the facilities because of overcrowding in their own premises. Probably most prominent among these were the buildings opposite Bellevue House, at what is now the north end of London Road. The barracks were later an orphanage and a riding school, and most famously the Ordnance Survey offices. Accommodation in the area was built in preparation for an expected influx of 10,000 French emigrants and troops from elsewhere overseas. In the meantime, the new buildings were used by regiments coming and going as part of the war effort – on the understanding that new arrivals would take priority when they landed. Stationed just outside the town were the York Hussars, the Duke of York's regiment.

The early exchanges of the war, however, ended largely ignominiously for the British, and the likelihood of invasion from across the Channel increased. Predictably, in the summer of 1796, resorts along the south coast temporarily became less attractive as leisure destinations. The quiet period at least allowed Southampton to be seen for itself without the majority of tourists. As an observer reflected, 'the gentility of the inhabitants of the town and its environs can form a more splendid assembly than many public places even at the height of their season'. It was in 1796's climate of quietude that an auxiliary army was created, consisting of civilians who would undergo military training and thereafter be liable for deployment to any part of the country that was in need. Accordingly, in early 1797, the Southampton Volunteer Cavalry came into being, comprising over fifty of the town's traders under the command of a Captain Smith, who pledged their active loyalty at a time of 'perilous crisis'.

There then followed three troops of volunteer infantry, the first of which was known as the Southampton Volunteers. A further corps was founded by Walter Taylor, who owned the Navy Block Manufactory at Wood Mill. His business was described at the time as 'a flourishing concern', and his wealth enabled him to finance the operation entirely. Since Taylor lived at Portswood Green, the troop was christened the Portswood Green Volunteers, and it was commanded by Samuel Taylor, Walter's son. Lastly, the Associated Householders were led by Sir Yelverton Peyton, mayor in 1791 and 1799, who collected volunteers from the town's 'very respectable tradesmen'. The total volunteer force numbered between 300 and 400 men, and their presence must have offered some solace to the worried townspeople: in the spring of 1798, rumours abounded of an impending invasion from across the Channel. The French were reported to be assembling vessels along their north coast, and Napoleon was known to be in Dunkirk, frantically directing mysterious operations. Sightings of unfamiliar ships were regular causes of suspicion and fear, and anxiety was exacerbated by the lack of armaments supplied to coastal defences.

Fortunately, the dreaded invasion never came and Nelson's victory at Copenhagen in 1801 decreased the likelihood that it ever would. With the Peace of Amiens in 1802 came a short period of harmony, but conflict returned the following year. At the outbreak of peace, the various volunteer corps had been disbanded, but they soon rose to the new challenge and were merged into a single unit called the Loyal Southampton Fusiliers. New recruits needed little incentive to join, but incentive was abundant if they did. Napoleon revived his threat to 'jump the ditch' and invade, while propaganda posters in Southampton (and elsewhere) were rife – Shakespeare's lines from *Henry V* and grim warnings about the aftermath of capitulation to the French stirred Southampton's men into action. The troops were commanded by Josias Jackson, the owner of Bellevue House, who would later become one of the town's MPs. As an additional line of protection, Southampton benefited from a waterborne band of volunteers known as the Sea Fencibles. Nationally the uptake was equally impressive: by 1804, just short of 400,000 men had volunteered, almost half the defence force for the entire country.

Compared with the previous decade, however, the number of official troops in and around Southampton was small – a nominal presence to support the volunteer forces if required. The spirits of the townspeople were boosted by the visit of the king and queen (and other members of the royal family) in October 1804, when they were received at the Audit House. A year later, there was a turning point in the war (at least in terms of morale) with the famous victory at Trafalgar. Towards the end of the battle, with Nelson dead, Admiral Collingwood took over the role of commander-in-chief, and, with his own ship badly damaged, he transferred his flag to *Euryalus*. Thus, a victory still considered one of the greatest in the history of the British armed forces ended with the head of the fleet at the helm of a ship built in Bucklers Hard in 1803. As at many other towns, the success was celebrated in Southampton, with special commemorative illuminations on two evenings in November.

The town's social scene, perhaps surprisingly, survived the ongoing conflicts. Visitors still arrived in good numbers, and the waterfront walk known as the Beach was 'graced every evening' with finely dressed ladies keen to take the sea air. Excitement among the elite was stirred when John Henry Petty purchased the decrepit castle site in 1804. Petty, the eldest son of former Prime Minister William Petty FitzMaurice, had himself been an MP and would become Marquis of Lansdowne upon his father's death. He funded the renovations through the sale of his father's valuable book collection, which realised nearly £7,000 from a month-long sale in 1806, and the next year a folio of manuscripts was sold to the British Museum for nearly £5,000.

The castle was virtually unrecognisable from the defensive bastion of years gone by. Some time after the Civil War, the land had been 'parcelled out to several people who have built houses and made gardens upon the ground'. Subsequently a windmill had been built on the hill (as depicted in an engraving of 1723); this was later adapted to become a summer house. By the time Petty purchased the castle site from a Mr Watson, the bulk of the ancient keep had been removed, but the little that remained was incorporated into the new building – 'an extensive castellated mansion of brick and stucco' in an ostentatious gothic style. The workmanship, however, may have left something to be desired. Moy Thomas, a young man travelling the south-west of England, observed that, 'The tower and upper part of the building have a very fine appearance … but when you approach near the tout-ensemble has a poor appearance. The lower part is not nearly finished.' Furthermore, the 'castle' was little benefited by its location, 'surrounded by mean little hovels occupied by the lowest description of poor people', according to Thomas.

Nevertheless, the marquis (as he became in 1805) entertained the town's nobility at lavish gatherings that became high points on the social calendar. In August 1807, for example, Lansdowne hosted a Race Week Ball including

A View of the Marquis of Lansdownes Castle, Southampton

In the early nineteenth century, the remains of the castle were adapted and rebuilt by the Marquis of Lansdowne.

a meal for 300 guests, leading to congestion in the streets around the castle. From her rented home in Castle Square, well removed from the 'mean little hovels', Jane Austen overlooked the comings and goings at the Lansdownes' peculiar residence. Their unorthodox tastes were evidently not limited to their home, since Austen recorded seeing them driven in a small carriage pulled by eight ponies manned by liveried staff. After three years in Southampton, the Austens moved to Chawton, in 1809, and in November that year the death of the marquis also curtailed the life of his curious abode. His bereaved wife, Mary Maddox, stayed in Southampton for two further years and remained a prominent socialite, but the 'castle' was later sold and eventually demolished in 1818. The original castle mound was reduced in size and was subsequently occupied by the Zion chapel, which in all probability removed any surviving traces of the Norman keep.

The Marquis of Lansdowne's gothic castle folly may have been short-lived, but he left another longer lasting contribution to the town. Before his death, in 1809, he had donated a statue of King George III, inspired by a likeness of the Emperor Hadrian held in the British Museum, to be installed on the Bargate facing south down the High Street. It was put in place in September 1809, replacing a statue of Queen Anne, but its donor only lived to see it for a further two months.

⚜

As described by Moy Thomas the following year, Southampton was evidently still in fine fettle – 'a large and respectable town, very clean and of a pleasing appearance'. 'Sweeter spots for elegant residence but few places in England can boast of,' continued Thomas, observing that the social elite who continued to frequent the town lent it 'a high reputation as a watering place of elegant and fashionable resort'. Slowly, but surely, Southampton was also by this time expanding beyond the old town walls. The defensive ditches outside the Bargate had been done away with – filled in during the second half of the eighteenth century. The quality and sturdiness of the buildings in Above Bar Street had improved, although they were still relatively few in number and almost exclusively adjacent to the main thoroughfare itself.

Further north, New Road was built running east from Above Bar Street towards the bridge erected at Northam in 1799, which enhanced the town's links with Portsmouth and Sussex. Close to this junction was a new row of grand houses known as Moira Place, commemorating the name of Lord Moira whose troops had assembled at and departed from Southampton in the 1790s. Beyond Moira Place, additional elegant new residences were taking shape on the roads running east and west from what is now the very northern end of Above Bar Street. Again, their names came from contemporary figures – Cumberland Place immortalised the Duke of Cumberland, George III's youngest son, while Brunswick Place denoted an alternate name for the royal house of Hanover.

More intense urbanisation was taking place along the portion of East Street that extended beyond the old town walls, referred to as Lower East Street in a map of 1791. Hanover Buildings branched out to the north and Spring Gardens to the south, while East Street itself led towards St Mary's church, which had for many years been somewhat isolated from the main part of the town. Otherwise, the area between Lower East Street and the coast was still sparsely populated.

The area within the town walls was showing signs of redevelopment and modernisation – a reflection of the affluence brought to the town by the popularity of its spa waters. The charming Tudor-style timber-framed buildings in the High Street had either been replaced or given new brick or stone frontages, giving the street cleaner lines and a more orderly appearance. Improvements had also taken place at the southern end of the High Street, close to the waterside and Town Quay. Following the appointment of the Pier and Harbour Commission in 1803, the Water Gate, already in a decrepit state, was finally demolished. Access to Town Quay was thus significantly eased and 'a fine view of the river and the New Forest' was created. The West Quay, which also fell under the administration of the Commissioners after 1803, was in a similarly poor condition, and was sold in 1810. These enhancements served to perpetuate Southampton's attractiveness to visitors: in 1812, poet and dramatist, Mary Mitford effusively described the town as one with 'an airiness, an animation, which might become the capital of Fairyland'. However, the fashion for spa water and bathing would not last indefinitely and the town would have to look elsewhere to grow and progress further.

HENRY CHARLES ENGLEFIELD

A man to whom anyone researching the history of Southampton owes a debt of gratitude is Sir Henry Charles Englefield. Born in 1752, Englefield devoted the majority of his life to study and writing, covering a wide range of interests, and before he was thirty, he had joined the Royal Society (reputedly the oldest scientific institution in the world) and the Society of Antiquaries. In 1801, he completed his work, *A Walk Through Southampton*, in which he visited many of the town's locations and recorded his observations, much as architectural historian Nikolaus Pevsner would do in the twentieth century. On occasion, Englefield theorised over historical details, although, as he modestly conceded, this was 'a task for which neither my researches nor abilities have by any means qualified me'. Nevertheless, his writings provided an invaluable snapshot of Southampton at the turn of the nineteenth century, particularly of some of the Roman remains at Bitterne and the Norman buildings in the oldest part of the town, which quickly deteriorated in the following decades. Without Englefield's diligence, much knowledge may have been lost. His work, when published, also featured a number of fascinating engravings, which offer further insight into the appearance of Southampton at the time, including images of Roman antiquities and even Netley Abbey. Englefield's other writings saw him tackle a study of the Isle of Wight and the demolition and replacement of London Bridge. The latter work was completed in 1821, the year before Englefield died.

In 1841, John Bullar produced a revised edition of *A Walk Through Southampton*, and wrote of its original author: 'The range of his attainments was very extensive, yet not the less accurate and profound. There was scarcely any branch of knowledge, either useful or ornamental, with which he was not familiarly conversant.'

eight

GROWTH & REFORM

Southampton's trade unsurprisingly suffered thanks to the conflicts in Europe. Following the positive developments of the 1780s commerce with France was naturally the most affected, but trade with other European countries was also depleted, whether because goods were forwarded through France or that other seaborne passages were considered hazardous as well. Once again, the business that Southampton traders conducted with the rest of Britain, Ireland and the Channel Islands became all-important.

Local industry was in an equally unspectacular state. Demand for the town's shipbuilding dropped away at the end of the war and the naval-block factory owned by Walter Taylor (founder of the Portswood Green Volunteers at the end of the previous century) fell victim to modernisation. Taylor, the third generation of a family of carpenters, had advanced methods of precision manufacturing, including the development of an early form of circular saw. His business had been extremely prosperous, thanks to lucrative orders from the Royal Navy to equip its fleet. Rather than move production to the yards of Portsmouth, Taylor convinced the Navy Board that his own mills would provide a better supply, keeping the industry in Southampton when it might have been lost. By 1781, the company had developed so much that it had outgrown its first home close to West Quay, and had been relocated to Wood Mill outside the town. Taylor's affluence was such that he was able to take up residence in the grand mansion Portswood Lodge, and he even provided a schoolroom for his employees' children. However, early in the new century his company faced stiff competition from Portsmouth Block Mills, which used machinery recently invented by Marc Isambard Brunel – a formidable engineer, but largely forgotten to history in favour of his son, Isambard Kingdom Brunel. The new equipment was designed in such a way that it required little skill to operate and produced an output ten times that achievable with the methods used at Wood Mill.

Taylor died in 1803, and his firm was soon unable to offer any meaningful competition in a field it had once dominated.

The only other significant industries in Southampton at the time were silk production and coach-building. The latter developed hand in hand with the tourist trade, becoming the town's leading manufacture.

The coming of peace brought with it an almost immediate increase in cross-Channel commerce. Although trade was initially unusually high, it settled at a level that was still considered significant. Business with the Baltic countries also resumed, and in time exceeded its pre-war levels. Timber from Norway, Sweden and Russia came into Southampton in great quantities, bound for London and other south-coast towns, including Poole, Weymouth, Chichester and Shoreham. The other regular and sizeable arrival in the port was coal from Tyneside, some of which was transported inland, while the rest was transferred to other vessels and taken to nearby coastal towns.

Economic improvements in Southampton's welfare were fortuitously timed. The administrators of the Corporation had lapsed into such a state of apathy that they barely bothered to fulfil some of their most fundamental duties. Records indicate that between 1815 and 1818 no financial statements detailing the town's accounts were issued at all. Furthermore, when the fiscal situation was finally revealed, in 1818, it showed a debt that would take six years to eradicate, requiring the mortgaging of the Audit House. An anonymous writer of 1816 may have 'hailed the houses of Above Bar as a delightful signal of what we should see in this thriving and fashionable place', but soon the town's popularity in the eyes of tourists dwindled somewhat. In 1817, the Spa Gardens were 'nearly deserted', and three years later, the spa water itself was only available in bottles at chemists' establishments in the town.

The grand evening balls at the Long Rooms, once events at which any self-respecting socialite wished to be seen, were so badly supported in 1819 and 1820 that they were only held sporadically. The situation improved in 1821 when Sir William Champion de Crespigny took over the running of the Long Rooms from the Martin family, whose association with the venue dated back nearly sixty years. The new owner was already a familiar figure in Southampton after serving as an MP for the previous two years, and under his stewardship, the Long Rooms experienced something of a renaissance. Recognising the bigger picture, de Crespigny also became involved in encouraging the provision of other entertainments and pastimes for the benefit of residents and tourists alike.

In late 1820, another significant development took place with the introduction of gas lighting to the town. After an initial flurry of activity that saw them address the most pressing problems of the early 1770s, the Paving, Lighting and Watching Commissioners had lapsed into a state of near inertia. Committee meetings often saw little business transacted, and occasionally none at all. Under such ineffective control, it is little surprise that Southampton's lighting became unreliable, with accusations of neglect made against the contractors responsible for maintaining the town's illumination. The improvements, when they came, were in no small part thanks to the generosity of William Chamberlayne, the town's second MP alongside Sir William Champion de Crespigny. Chamberlayne donated 'the iron pillars for supporting the public lights', a gift commemorated by the Corporation and townspeople with the purchase of the Chamberlayne Column in 1823. The new system did not immediately ease concerns about the diligence of the contractors, however: some back streets remained unlit while in other areas lamps were lighted too late and put out too early. By the end of the decade, by which time many shops in the High Street were also gas-lit, the majority of the problems had been ironed out.

Meanwhile, although the increase in cargo trade was undoubtedly good news for Southampton's economy after the lean war years, the other significant

Town Quay in the mid-nineteenth century, showing the Gas Column that commemorated William Chamberlayne's contribution to street lighting in Southampton.

development was the growing popularity of seaborne passenger routes. Vessels serving Le Havre had been busy in the decade before the French Revolution, and with the times of threat and anarchy now in the past, they resumed their trade. Closer to home, the Isle of Wight (and Cowes specifically) was also becoming popular as a tourist destination, and the Channel Islands once again attracted visitors who were reassured that their passage would be a safe one.

Unbeknown to those operating these services, the passenger trade held the key to Southampton's future as a port. The other important factor was the advent of steam-powered vessels, which were quicker than sailing ships and less reliant on favourable weather. Enhancing the benefits of the new motive force yet further, the navigation of Southampton Water in traditional sailing ships had been notoriously tricky; this became much easier with steam. The introduction of steamboats had been considered in 1815 – being rather understatedly described as a 'useful invention'. In 1820, the Prince Coburg, a paddle steamer of 24hp, began her career on the Isle of Wight route, three years after another steam ferry had first connected Portsmouth and Ryde. Two more steamers were soon added to the service shuttling across the Solent, and, in 1823, a steamer began regular service back and forth to Le Havre, to be joined by another such vessel the following year. At around the same time yet another steamer started to serve the Channel Islands, and pleasure cruises were introduced. These circled the Isle of Wight or journeyed to Brighton, which was itself enjoying a period of prosperity as a tourist destination. Among other such jollities, the Cowes Regatta of 1825 was served by two steamers that carried enthusiastic visitors, who enjoyed on-board catering and entertainment provided by a band.

Alongside this picturesque scene, Southampton was experiencing a final flourish as a spa resort, thanks at least in part to William Champion de Crespigny's rescue of the Long Rooms and his enthusiasm for developing 'the amusements of the town'. In the late 1820s, Southampton was a vibrant tourist trap once more, with newly added attractions such as balloon ascents and circuses joining established entertainments, including regattas and musical concerts. Times were good enough that new buildings began to spring up to serve the resort: the Royal Gloucester Baths and Promenade Rooms were opened close to Town Quay in 1829, while the following year new assembly rooms were also constructed. These were named the Royal Victoria Rooms in honour of Princess Victoria, who patronised a banquet held there shortly after they were first opened.

During this period, the town was frequented by A.B. Granville, a physician and traveller who toured the country recording his observations of spa resorts. Granville later noted his assertion that 'viewed under every possible aspect, Southampton offers to people with delicate lungs or irritable trachea a retreat preferable almost to those found on the south-western coast, including Torquay itself'. Perhaps because of these benefits, Southampton also became an attractive location for retirees at this time. In an era before the affluent began to winter in warmer Mediterranean climes, living in a villa or mansion in the town offered a salubrious and fashionable retirement. However, those who ventured further afield for one reason or another used the port in increasing numbers: by 1830, an estimated 100,000 passengers each year were making their journeys through Southampton. The trend was aided by the growing number of steamers, which were becoming larger and more efficient and charging ever more reasonable fares. In 1831, a crossing to Le Havre cost as little as 10s. Once across the Channel many travellers continued to Paris or elsewhere in France, or increasingly, Italy. The town, as A. Temple Patterson noted, 'was beginning to proclaim itself a gateway to the Continent'. Local economy was further boosted by the fact that most, if not all, of the sea-bound passengers would spend at least some time (and, therefore, money) in Southampton before their journeys.

The combination of the town's revival as a tourist resort and the increase in its passenger trade led to a growth in population similar, proportionately, to those seen in the industrialised centres in the North of England. The census of 1801 (which did not include the suburb of Portswood) recorded a residency of 7,913; thirty years later, this had expanded to 19,324. The growth naturally necessitated further new building, which predominantly occurred to the north, emanating from the central axis of Above Bar Street, and to the east. Not far beyond the old walls the impressive town houses of Portland Street and Portland Terrace sprang up – large and grand residences incorporating Classical design motifs, only within reach of the wealthy. Aimed at the equally affluent were the spacious houses to be found in Carlton Crescent and Rockstone Place, further north beyond the open space known as the Marlands. Carlton Crescent was enthusiastically described by Nikolaus Pevsner as 'the most spectacular piece of Regency development in Southampton'. The houses were fundamentally the same but differing in small ways, and Pevsner admired their 'austere elegance and economy of detail'. With the identity of their designer or designers unknown, he speculated that the architects responsible may have originated from (or at least worked in) Plymouth or Aberdeen, owing to the presence of similar buildings in those towns. These new residences would before long find themselves adjacent to the extremities of the suburb known as the Polygon, which itself was 'much resorted to by families of respectability and eminence'. To serve these new and expanding residential areas a small, localised shopping street developed. Bedford Place began to flourish in about 1820, providing the new homeowners of the district with an attractive row of shops featuring bow windows; these recalled Southampton's original retail thoroughfare, the High Street.

The most spectacular increase in population, however, took place in the St Mary's area of the town, which for many years had remained somewhat separate from the main hub of Southampton and had accordingly retained something of a rural atmosphere. Whereas the new residential suburbs to the north of the town had been built to attract the prosperous, St Mary's was very much aimed at the working class – 'labourers and mechanics' in the words of a newspaper from 1824. One of the contributory factors was the resurgence of the shipbuilding industry, which had declined sharply at the end of the Napoleonic Wars. The downturn had proved terminal for much of the trade based at West Quay, but the yards at Northam, despite a few fallow years, were to re-emerge. In 1824, construction began again at a number of yards there, and they were soon to be joined by John Rubie, who was already building yachts and other light craft further downriver. Five years later, Rubie would become Southampton's first shipbuilder to complete a steamship, when he launched the paddle steamer *Emerald*, which operated on the service to Hythe.

The population of St Mary's was exploding to say the least. From a figure of slightly over 4,700 in 1821, it grew to nearly 15,000 in the next twenty years. Alongside this growth, inevitably, came an increase in crime, not least because the expansion of the district had outstripped the jurisdiction of the Paving, Lighting and Watching Commissioners. There were no patrols conducted there by the watchmen and 'the town constables and their assistants rarely ventured to show their faces in Kingsland'. The class divide and social prejudice that would define the area for many years was already firmly in place: in 1831, the *Hampshire Advertiser* observed that it was 'inhabited by many disreputable elements'.

Southampton's growth was such that when the new king, William IV, was crowned in September 1831, the celebrations had to be more restrained than in previous years. A committee charged with taking care of the finances of the

Above The much admired Georgian town houses of Carlton Crescent, still glorious in 2011.

Right Looking south down Bedford Place in 2011, with the Civic Centre clock tower just visible in the distance.

festivities declared it 'impossible, from the increased population of the town, to give a public dinner, as at the last coronation'. Instead, church bells rang out across the town and a fireworks display was provided. Any fervent monarchists disappointed by this outcome only had to wait until the following month to be compensated by the visit of the Duchess of Kent and her daughter, Princess Victoria, who stayed at the Star Inn for a few days en route from Bath to Portsmouth. The royal visitors were received at the Audit House, where the duchess spoke in reply to an address made by the town recorder, after which she and the princess were introduced to members of the Corporation and the town's clergymen.

When the duchess and princess next came to Southampton, less than two years later, it was for a specific ceremonial occasion – the grand opening of the newly completed Royal Pier. The growth of the port's passenger trade in the previous decade had served to accentuate the poor quality of the embarking and landing facilities on offer: vessels had improved enormously in terms of speed and efficiency, while the quaysides remained largely unchanged. Passengers were faced with two potential levels of inconvenience: the first of these was the necessity to be transferred in a smaller boat to the ship on which they would make their main journey. At low tides, however, this paled into insignificance next to the alternative of wading across the mudbanks to reach or leave Town Quay.

Initial investigations into building a pier had begun as far back as 1805, when John Rennie had been asked 'to make a survey of the port and harbour for the purpose of giving a plan of improvement'. Rennie was a specialist in bridges and marine engineering projects, and would later be knighted for overseeing the completion of his father's design for London Bridge. On Rennie's recommendation, the emphatically named John Doswell Doswell was appointed surveyor to the Harbour Commissioners, a position he would hold for over half a century. Although Doswell was soon busy with the construction of sea walls and general improvements to the port's quaysides, the question of a pier was not meaningfully broached for several years. However, with the increase in the steamship trade in the 1820s, further pressure to build a pier came from the businessmen operating the routes. This resulted in a meeting of the townspeople in 1828, at which a committee was appointed to apply pressure to the Harbour Board.

In February 1831, Doswell was asked to present 'plans and estimates of a wooden and of a stone landing place'. The two options for the scheme were

The Pier, Southampton, at the turn of the century. (Library of Congress, LC-DIG-ppmsc-08849)

respectively priced at £7,500 and £14,000, and subsequently a timber construction was chosen with a budget of £10,000. That July, an Act of Parliament secured funds for the scheme, and the Harbour Commissioners thereafter became known as the Pier and Harbour Commissioners, reflecting the expanded scope of their responsibilities. The pier was constructed in six months under the supervision of an engineer named Mr Betts, and it was completed in the summer of 1833.

On 8 July, the Duchess of Kent and Princess Victoria visited Southampton to perform the opening ceremony, journeying from their temporary stay at Norris Castle in East Cowes. They arrived in the royal yacht, *Emerald*, and were greeted by a group of seven gentlemen, themselves on a barge displaying at its bow the badge of the town's admiralty; a silver oar. The duchess and princess alighted at the pier stairs, where they were met by the mayor and members of the Corporation. The scene was observed by around 25,000 spectators gathered for the event. The party retired to a marquee for refreshments, after which the town clerk formally invited the duchess to perform the opening.

She responded: 'It affords me great pleasure to name the pier "The Royal Pier", and I am to add our sincere good wishes that it may promote the prosperity of the town.' After this auspicious inauguration, however, the early life of the pier was somewhat troubled. In 1837, it was reported that the wooden supports were suffering 'the ravages of some marine insects', and before a further five years had elapsed, Doswell was forced to replace the foundations completely with new, protected timbers.

At the same time that the plans for the new pier were being made the construction of docks and a railway between Southampton and London were also under discussion – a project that, like the pier, would take several years to come to fruition. 'Railway mania' was spreading across the country: in September 1830, the world's first steam-operated double-tracked railway opened between Liverpool and Manchester, and throughout the land, other schemes were already afoot. In Southampton that same year a private meeting to debate the idea of a rail link to the capital was held at the home of Abel Dottin, one of the town's MPs. A committee was formed, including in its number Lieutenant-Colonel George Henderson, who had also been one of the prominent members of the committee created in 1828 to liaise with the Harbour Board over the pier scheme.

The colonel travelled to London to find an engineer able to undertake the scheme and, on a recommendation, approached Francis Giles. Giles had been educated under the tutelage of John Rennie and had worked with him on a number of canal projects. He had made the transition to rail with the Newcastle–Carlisle line, work on which would run concurrently with the London–Southampton route. In 1830, Giles made a general survey of the land likely to be used, and considered routes via either Guildford or Basingstoke, the latter being subsequently selected. Giles was officially appointed engineer in 1831, and in April that year the Southampton and London Railway and Dock Company was formed after a positive public meeting.

Henderson took his place as chairman of the company, which was set up in order to facilitate the landing of goods at the port and their smooth onward journey to the capital by rail. The advantages, it was hoped, would be looked on especially enthusiastically by merchants whose routes entered the English Channel from the west, who would save significant time and expense through not having to negotiate the narrowest part of the Channel and the Thames Estuary. With memories of the Napoleonic Wars still fresh, vessels would also be less exposed to potential attack. Most coveted was the lucrative West Indian trade, with any reduction in the lengthy transatlantic crossing times seen as worthwhile. British consumption of sugar, by way of example, would double between 1800 and 1850. Henderson declared, 'I confess I cannot comprehend how such manifold and manifest advantages can fail to produce their hitherto unvaried results.'

Initially, however, financial support for the scheme proved difficult to garner, and after due consideration the company made the decision to concentrate its efforts on the railway rather than the docks. Had it not been for the diligence and hard work of Lieutenant-Colonel Henderson, this aspect of the project might too have foundered: he travelled far and wide, from London to Scotland, in an attempt to drum up the monetary backing required, and eventually achieved his aims. Ultimately, an incredible 40 per cent of the capital raised came from concerns not in either Southampton or London, but in Manchester. Construction of the railway was confirmed when the associated Act of Parliament was given royal assent, in July 1834, authorising the building of a line 'commencing at the River Thames, at or near Nine Elms … to the shore or beach at or near a place called the Marsh in the parish of St Mary in the town and county town of Southampton.' Southampton Corporation acquired the necessary land for the new scheme and, after years of debate, planning and preparation, work on the line finally began in October 1834.

Another significant development was in progress – one that would truly, and irrevocably, change the face of Southampton. In 1832, the Reform Act eradicated most of the country's infamous, rotten electoral boroughs. The introduction of the legislation was greeted in Southampton with 'great rejoicing' the streets were decorated with flags, a band performed and church bells rang out across the town. The same week an enormous feast was provided in the High Street, attended by over 3,000 of the townspeople. However, the first general election under the new Act, held in December that year, did little to dispel the controversies of old, at least in Southampton. James Barlow Hoy, one of the trustees of the Railway and Dock Company, first elected after the death of William Chamberlayne, won the election by a majority of only ten votes. However, the result aroused such suspicion that Parliament was petitioned to overturn it. The ensuing enquiry upheld the petitioners' claim, and the previously defeated Whig candidate, John Storey Penleaze (a director of the Railway and Dock Company) was declared elected instead. Whig supporters who had distanced themselves from the challenge to the original result felt able to show their colours, and celebrated the victory at a special dinner. Ultimately, the incident illustrated the defeat of the corruption that had tainted both Southampton and the rest of the country. 'At no period,' observed the *Hampshire Advertiser*, 'has any event occasioned a greater excitement in the town.'

As a continuation of the efforts that led to the passing of the Reform Act, the execution and, in many cases, integrity of local government across the nation also came under review. A small number of boroughs were investigated in 1833, and Southampton was visited by two representatives of the Commission of Enquiry into Municipal Corporations. In some other areas, the enquiries were met with suspicion, fear and even outright obstruction, as corporations sought to distract attention from the abuses of power that were often alarmingly prevalent. Southampton, however, offered no such resistance, with the Commissioners given 'every assistance in their investigations'. This acquiescence may have been because of the Corporation's confidence that it had little or nothing to hide. At the end of the enquiries, no significant criticisms or accusations were made, although the Commissioners pointed out the town's apparent lack of ambition and its reticence towards trying new things. Compared with some other boroughs (where, for example, the mayor's role was effectively meaningless, or where public money was spent on feasts for Corporation members), Southampton's faults were tame to say the least.

Over the course of two years, a royal commission investigated nearly 300 towns and set about making its recommendations. When the Municipal Reform Act was passed in September 1835, it affected 178 boroughs across the country. Southampton was divided into five wards, roughly based on the town's five parishes. Each ward was to be represented by councillors elected by its residents – All Saints' with twelve and St Mary's with nine, while Holy Rood, St Michael's and St Lawrence's had three each. These thirty council members would have three-year tenures in their roles, although ten would be required to retire each year. Ten aldermen would also serve on the Council, elected by the councillors for a period of six years – again, a certain proportion would retire regularly – and every November the aldermen and councillors would elect the mayor. To avoid lapses of conscientiousness like those between 1815 and 1818, the Corporation's finances were to be audited regularly, and the accounts made available to the public, whose rates contributed part of the Council's income.

The area to the east of the River Itchen remained beyond Southampton's borough boundary (and thus also beyond its jurisdiction), but communication to the region improved in 1836 with the opening of a floating bridge. A scheme had first been proposed in 1833 when Francis Giles, the engineer working on the Southampton–London railway line, submitted plans for 'a swing bridge of seventeen arches'. There was, however, significant opposition to the idea, both from the local fishermen and the owners of the Northam Bridge – the latter group fearing that their toll bridge, which had opened just before the turn of the century, would suffer in the wake of new competition. When the Admiralty also joined the debate, warning about difficulties in navigating the river with such a bridge in place, a new design of chain-secured floating bridge was suggested. The system had been devised by engineer, James Meadows Rendel, whose first such ferry began operation in Dartmouth in 1832. A bill incorporating the new plans was submitted to Parliament, which, after further objection from the Northam Bridge Company, was passed in July 1834. The bridge was constructed in Devon, and upon its completion, in late 1836, was towed to Southampton by a steamer. It was formally opened, on 23 November, with a special inaugural crossing, including the mayor among its passengers. As well as the bridge itself, the scheme also allowed for new roads nearby and a striking entrance building on the western shore, at a total cost of over £35,000.

The mid-1830s were unquestionably a time that would define both Southampton's past and its future. With the old Corporation system reformed and the town's days as a tourist resort fading, one era was seemingly to coming to an end, with new projects such as the pier, railway and docks ushering in a modern age. As Lieutenant-Colonel Henderson had enthusiastically observed: 'A brighter day is dawning for Southampton; and it is to be hoped that the clouds which have for so long hung over her commercial horizon will soon be dispersed.'

WILLIAM CHAMBERLAYNE

Apart from his legacy to Southampton in the form of his contribution towards the town's public lighting, William Chamberlayne was remembered for leading a varied life both in and out of Parliament. Chamberlayne was the son of a lawyer and upon his father's death, in 1799, inherited the grand Coley Park estate in Berkshire and Weston Park, near Southampton. The following year, he became an MP for the first time, taking up a seat in Christchurch that he held for nearly two years. Around this time, he made the acquaintance of William Cobbett, a promoter of democratic reform whose campaigning in part led to the reshaping of the country's electoral system in later years. In 1802, Chamberlayne built Weston Grove House on his Southampton estate, and, in 1810, added an obelisk constructed as a memorial to Charles James Fox, the Whig politician remembered for his rivalry with William Pitt the Younger. Additionally, Fox was renowned for his libertarian standpoint – he fought against the slave trade and like Cobbett campaigned for parliamentary reform. Chamberlayne was elected as MP for Southampton in a by-election of March 1818, despite being described by Lord Malmesbury a few months earlier as 'a clever, half mad man, and not very correct in any of his principles'. Nevertheless, Chamberlayne remained in the role for the rest of his life, winning a further three election victories. The memorial column erected in his name was moved in 1829 from its original position on the corner of Northam Bridge Road to Town Quay, and again in 1860 to the southern end of the town's park near Hanover Buildings, where it remains today. Chamberlayne, despite his enthusiasm for parliamentary reform, was never a regular sight in the House, and he died in December 1829.

nine

RAILWAY & DOCKS

The new era that Lieutenant-Colonel Henderson eagerly foresaw was defined by the accession of Queen Victoria in the summer of 1837. William IV died on 20 June and his niece thus became the country's new monarch. The event was formally proclaimed in Southampton two days later, with announcements given outside the Bargate and at the Audit House. Victoria's reign saw enhancements in industry and technology that eclipsed any previous age, and, as in many other areas of the country, Southampton's future was further shaped in these years.

With construction of the new rail link to London underway, attention returned to the improvement and development of Southampton's docks. The projects went on to be heavily interdependent – they were, after all, originally considered as two parts of a single grand scheme. Those using the docks required an efficient transport route to the capital, and, without the increased traffic entering the port, the railway would be an expensive white elephant. A collective of businessmen had gathered to discuss the plans in 1834 and they presented their ideas to the Harbour Commissioners. They consulted the engineer William Cubitt (later heavily involved in the plans for the Crystal Palace built for the Great Exhibition of 1851), but their proposals were twice rejected by the Commissioners. Nonetheless, in 1836 a joint stock company was created by Act of Parliament with the expressed intention of building the new docks, the location of which would be the mudlands at the southern tip of the peninsula between the Test and Itchen rivers. Rather than Cubitt, appointed as engineer for the project was none other than Francis Giles, securing his second Southampton scheme while already deeply immersed in work on the rail link to London.

Once again, finances for the docks needed to be raised in the capital, but this fundamental obstacle was not the only one that the project faced. Some of the dissenting voices came from the councillors representing the Radical party, wary that financial support from the capital would give Londoners an inappropriate level of control over the port, especially as the company was so new and thus of unproven trustworthiness. Perhaps surprisingly, opposition was also raised by the Pier and Harbour Commissioners, who were concerned that Southampton's existing quays and the still relatively new Royal Pier would quickly become obsolete. Other opponents thought that the Corporation had failed to negotiate a good price for the mudlands: over 200 acres were sold for £5,000, with the sale completed in January 1837.

The objections, however, were eventually overcome, and, in 1838, work began on the docks with a budget of £1 million. On Friday, 12 October 1838 the ceremonial stone laying was held, beginning with a service at All Saints' church, from where a grand procession made its way down the High Street to the dock site. The ceremony was, as was the fashion at the time, conducted with full Masonic honours. Performing the task was Sir Lucius Curtis, the Deputy Provincial Grand Master of Hampshire, who had served in the Napoleonic Wars and would later become Admiral of the Fleet. Curtis was accompanied by Joseph Liggins, the chairman of the Southampton Dock Company, and also in attendance were the company directors, the mayor and Corporation members and a 'distinguished assembly', all overlooked by a crowd of around 20,000 people. The foundation stone itself consisted of two sections, one laid by Curtis and the other (the lower part), containing a commemorative plate and a selection of coins.

While work on the docks continued, progress with the rail link that would play such a vital role in the scheme was less encouraging. By February 1836, almost two years since the passing of the Act of Parliament, a mere 10 miles of line had been finished. This apparent lack of advancement created some consternation among the company's shareholders, who voiced their doubts that Francis Giles could be relied upon to give accurate quotes for the budget and timescale of the scheme. The engineer did little to allay these fears by announcing a huge increase in his estimates. In a declaration that must have caused enormous concern to the Dock Company, he conceded that the original budget of £1m at inception had expanded to over £1.5m by November 1836. For example, the cost of the land was initially estimated at £65,000, but would eventually exceed this figure by over £200,000. Giles's position became even less secure when Joseph Locke was asked to inspect the progress thus far and to submit his own plans and estimates for finishing the job. Locke had significant experience of working on major railway schemes, often including the need to overcome difficult obstacles. He was on good terms with both Isambard Kingdom Brunel

The ceremony at which the foundation stone of Southampton Docks was laid, in October 1838.

and Robert Stephenson, and, in fact, had been on the footplate of Stephenson's famous Rocket locomotive at the opening of the Liverpool–Manchester railway in 1830. More importantly, Locke was renowned for completing his works within or very close to budget.

Early in 1837, the inevitable transpired. Giles was relieved of his duties and Locke was appointed in his place. The new engineer quickly set about rectifying the difficulties that his predecessor had created and then allowed to fester. Locke reviewed the performances of the contractors and replaced those that had been underachieving. These actions, coupled with his experience and authoritarian manner, meant that Locke's appointment quickly paid dividends, and clear evidence of construction was soon evident. Only half a year into his tenure, he announced to the company directors that the line between London and Woking would be open at the start of May 1838. A cruel winter delayed this estimate marginally, but public passengers began to use the service on 21 May and, before long, about 1,000 people per day were making the journey. With Locke's practices now in fullest effect work proceeded apace. By June 1839, the line reached as far south as Basingstoke and northbound it joined Southampton and Winchester.

In the same month Southampton Station (later known as Southampton Terminus) was opened, although it was not used fully until the entire line to

London was finished. It was sited close to the nascent docks for easy access upon their completion, but was, nevertheless, 'amidst fields where cattle still grazed'. A striking building in the Italianate style, its architect was Sir William Tite, who went on to design London's Royal Exchange and act as President of the Royal Institute of British Architects. Although it was closed to passengers in 1966, the Terminus station is now hailed as one of the best examples of early railway architecture, and it influenced a number of other stations in the region, several of which were also designed by Tite. For another year, however, the interim journey between Winchester and Basingstoke required the use of horse-drawn transport, until the line was fully operational.

The first train to make the entire journey did so on Monday, 11 May 1840. Twenty-one empty carriages arrived in Southampton from London in the early hours of the morning, pulled by two engines. At 6.30 a.m., the first northbound train left for the capital, while at 8 a.m. the railway company's directors and their guests departed from London's Nine Elms station. They arrived on the south coast at 11.30 a.m. (thus taking thirty minutes longer than the fastest regular service would), to be greeted at the Terminus station by a civic deputation. The following month the completion of the project was celebrated in Southampton with a grand gala dinner on 20 June. The event was held in a marquee on the Royal Victoria Archery Ground and was attended by 600 people. Among the distinguished guests were future Prime Minister Lord Palmerston and the French ambassador – the latter arriving by train from Nine Elms in the early afternoon and returning to London that evening. The final cost of the project was close to Giles's revised 1836 estimate of £1.5m; Joseph Locke's invaluable contribution ensured this was not exceeded further.

Predictably, the rail service sounded a virtual death knell for the coach routes between Southampton and London. Thirteen coaches daily had travelled each way in 1838, with the journey taking around eight hours, but within three years of the advent of rail only one coach operator survived, hoping to attract its customers by offering a leisurely trip for 'those to whom time is no object'. Four years later, this last service had also fallen by the wayside, and the only coach routes remaining were those connecting towns not yet joined by rail. By association, the town's coach manufacturing industry was also badly affected, although there was still some demand for privately owned carriages, and a steady growth in overseas trade helped to soften the blow.

Meanwhile, Southampton's shipbuilding trade continued to be healthy following its revival in the mid-1820s. Indicative of this was the relocation from

Millbrook to Northam of the Summers, Groves & Day engineering company in 1840. For the previous ten years, the firm had run an ironworks, its location to be commemorated in later years by the naming of Foundry Lane. In 1836, Summers, Groves & Day had built and launched the first iron ship made in Southampton: *Forester* was 65ft in length and was designed to operate on a shuttle service to Hythe. Three years later, the company had supplied a 10hp railway locomotive to be used in trials on the Southampton–Winchester line, and subsequently a larger and more powerful engine, which formed part of the passenger service. After expanding its output, the decision was taken to move the company to Northam, the advantages of which were numerous. As well as the obvious rail connection with London, there was also a network of tramways to distribute necessary materials when they arrived. Additionally the potential workforce of St Mary's was close by, but the adjacent Northam area itself was soon increasing in population too, with 'land laid out for streets and a general scene of bustle'.

As well as being the year when a rail link connected Southampton to the capital, 1840 was also when the Peninsular and Oriental Company selected Southampton as its centre of operations. P&O (as it is more popularly known) had won a contract with the government to carry mail to the east and had been incorporated by a royal charter with an initial budget of £1m. The company originally intended to have its headquarters in Falmouth, but a number of logistical problems led to a change of heart. The Royal Mail had chosen a base in Falmouth, but despite this, and advice from the Treasury, P&O opted for Southampton taking into account the new docks and associated rail link. The company's mail service route to Alexandria began in June 1840, operating from the Royal Pier until the new dock was finished. Construction work soon gathered pace and, in 1841, nearly 2,000 men were employed on the scheme, managing to excavate 25,000 cubic yards of material every week. The first dock, later known as the Outer Dock, was first used in the summer of 1842, costing around £140,000. At the time, it was the largest dock in England, covering an area of 16 acres and with an entrance measuring 150ft across, through which water first flowed in May of that year. At low tide, the water was 18ft deep and the average tidal differential was 13ft. The dock was officially opened on 29 August 1842 when two P&O vessels, *Liverpool* and *Tagus*, entered it, becoming the first ships to arrive at Southampton and unload their cargoes directly onto the newly built rail link to London. Packages arriving in Southampton at 9 a.m., it was boasted, would be in the capital by 2 p.m. For those observing the scene there could have been no clearer indication of the benefits of the combined rail and docks development.

The new railway line had already been graced by royal patronage when William IV's widow, Queen Adelaide, journeyed from Nine Elms to Southampton in June 1842. The following year, the scheme received a further unofficial royal seal of approval when, on 28 August 1843, Queen Victoria and Prince Albert arrived by train, having set out from Windsor. The queen and prince were accompanied by the Duke of Wellington, who had previously been reticent about travelling by rail, despite being provided with a train specifically for his own personal use. Upon reaching the Terminus station, the royal party was met by Major-General Sir H. Pakenham and his staff, along with the mayor and members of the Corporation. At the pier, Victoria and Albert were rejoined by the Duke of Wellington 'and other noble personages' before continuing their journey to France and Belgium.

The Royal Mail later moved its headquarters to Southampton in 1843, the government having reconsidered its previous position. Influential in the decision was an investigative report into the suitability of the docks; this bore the cumbersome but transparent title 'Southampton as a Steam Boat Station is Unrivalled in England'. In spring 1845, work began on the port's first graving (dry) dock. Construction was completed the following summer at a cost of around £60,000 and the dock was officially opened in July 1846, 400ft in length with an entrance nearly 70ft wide. In 1847, a second, smaller dry dock was completed, enabling Southampton to offer the sort of possibilities for ship repairs previously reserved for London and Portsmouth. Once again, the business advantages were clear: merchants could now unload London-bound cargoes and have their vessels repaired in the same port. Adjacent to the docks were the expected cranes and related equipment, as well as bountiful warehousing facilities. Soon there was 10 miles of railway line on the quaysides alone to manoeuvre the goods as efficiently as possible. 'Cargoes of every description are landed and warehoused,' it was observed, 'or forwarded by railway with great expedition, there existing from the dock quays and warehouses perfect and rapid railway communication to all parts of the metropolis, the coalfields, and manufacturing districts.'

Southampton was already seeing the benefits of this investment in the docks and rail link. In 1845, the port had been the fifth busiest in the country when ranked in terms of the number of inbound and outbound vessels, their combined tonnage and the value of British and Irish goods exported –

nearly £1.5 million. The only other ports exceeding these levels of trade at the time were London, Liverpool, Hull and Glasgow, and by the following year, the value of Southampton's exports had doubled to almost £3m. The new developments also brought with them a small fillip to the town's tourist trade in the form of rail and sea excursions, which had begun as early as 1841. Hundreds of passengers made the journey from Nine Elms on a special train, transferring on arrival to a pleasure cruiser, which sailed around the Isle of Wight, returning to London in the early evening.

In 1846, the Southampton Emigration and Shipping Company was created. Its general manager was John Marshall, whose firm had been made the Dock Company's preferred commercial and shipping agents. In the wake of Southampton's selection as the departure point for emigrants to Canada, Marshall & Co. set up merchant services to Montreal and Quebec, and, in 1846, the new Emigration and Shipping Company also won the contract to run the emigration routes to Australia. Initially, however, the company performed poorly, until it gained great succour from the boom in traffic due to the Australian gold rush in the early 1850s.

While business at the docks continued to be strong in general, it perhaps failed to fulfil the over-ambitious expectations expressed when the scheme was initiated. Nevertheless, a further important development took place with the construction of the Southampton–Dorchester railway line, which opened up a large catchment area of trade to the west. A company had been formed to build the line in 1844, and originally intended to run it along the coast of Western Shore, terminating at a station close to the pier and Town Quay. Connection to the existing Terminus station would have been by means of a tram service, but this part of the scheme produced an objection from the Pier and Harbour Commissioners. The plans were duly altered and the new station was sited at the western end of a tunnel travelling under the Marlands, through which the railway line continued to meet the existing London line in Northam. After two years of construction, the line and station were completed and opened in 1847.

With unfortunate timing, the link to Dorchester became operational at the start of a period of economic depression. However, Southampton did not suffer as badly as some other parts of the country, and, in fact, achieved the acclaim of becoming the home port of Brunel's famous ship SS *Great Western*. The vessel, which had reduced the time of an Atlantic crossing to a new low of around a fortnight, had become part of the Royal Mail Steam Packet Company fleet and was used on the West Indies route for the next eight years. Furthermore, local trade was boosted after a reduction in freight charges at the docks, following a series of protests from unhappy businessmen.

No sooner had this turbulence begun to fade than another even greater challenge presented itself. London had been blighted by an outbreak of cholera in the early 1830s, leading to nearly 7,000 deaths, but the epidemic that began in 1848 was to be far more widespread. With the disease escalating, a committee was formed in Southampton in an attempt to prepare the town for the seemingly inevitable. The committee consisted in part of local physicians and members of the Council, who decided to divide the town into sixteen segments to facilitate effective management of the outbreak when it occurred. The first case was recorded on 17 June 1849, and a little over three months later, the death toll in Southampton stood at nearly 250. Fatalities were found in every part of the town, but, as may be expected, the poorer areas were the worst affected. The slum districts behind the becoming façades of the High Street either had rudimentary sewage systems or none at all, and some privies had been left unemptied for years.

Of perhaps equally great concern to the Corporation was the impact of the epidemic on the town's trade, which was at a virtual standstill until the end of September 1849. A suggestion was made (and endorsed by the Council) that an application should be submitted to Parliament to increase the town's ability to collect rates in order to finance the battle against cholera. This apparently cold-hearted solution, which would have punished the townspeople already suffering the ramifications of the outbreak, was understandably opposed in many quarters and an alternative answer was sought. The 1848 Public Health Act had created a centralised Board of Health, which in turn was able to create subsidiary local boards upon the submission of a petition signed by 10 per cent of the rate-paying inhabitants. In Southampton, this possibility was soon explored by several leading residents who were unencumbered by roles within the Council or any other body directly involved in the issue. Chief among these was a Captain Engledue, who had served on P&O vessels before becoming the company's representative superintendent at Southampton's port. Engledue's concerns were probably driven as much by business as by humanity: many of P&O's staff lived locally and illness and death among them was having an impact on the company's ability to trade effectively.

The port's medical practitioner, Dr Moore, undertook his own investigation into the root of the problem and came to some revealing conclusions. Among the key factors identified were the poor provision of drainage and sewage systems, the questionable quality of the water supply and a prevalence of stagnant cesspools. Additionally the poorer parts of the town were densely populated – crowded homes in narrow, dirty alleyways with little ventilation. Within an area of only ½ sq. mile in the district around French Street, for example, there were over 600 homes housing 3,200 people. The majority of Southampton's other physicians agreed emphatically with Moore's opinions, and laboured tirelessly to help the afflicted as best they could. One of these was Dr Francis Cooper, who had become prominent in local politics in the 1830s and would later be the first doctor in Southampton to die from cholera.

In the meantime, Captain Engledue's petition to the Central Board of Health was not garnering the level of local support that its originator may have hoped for. A public meeting was held, at which a majority vote considered the town able to deal with the situation without the need to avail itself of the Public Health Act. However, the Board of Health exercised its right to send an inspector to the town to make his own assessment and William Ranger duly arrived to undertake the task. He made observations of scenes that, thankfully, seem unthinkable today: 'In each place at the time of my inspection, there were accumulations of ashes, animal and vegetable refuse, in corners of premises, upon the surface of the yards, in cellars, and in some few instances in ash pits.' Elsewhere, however, conditions were even worse: 'In some instances the people have no privy accommodation of any kind; in others, as many as forty four and seventy four persons use a single privy in common. The privies are generally close to the dwellings, the walls in many cases saturated with foetid fluid, in some instances flowing on the floors of rooms occupied by families.'

Ranger's enquiry lasted twelve days and included testimony from many of Southampton's doctors as well as a number of the more prominent townspeople. His subsequent report was enough to convince the Central Board that the town's petition was a worthy one, but opposition was raised to the formation of a local board because of the perception that it would be funded by increased rates. A stand-off was avoided when Joseph Stebbing intervened. A man known as an 'invaluable solver of differences', Stebbing proposed that expenditure on addressing the town's health problems should be limited to £27,000, and with this proviso in place, a compromise was reached whereby the board's role would be incorporated into the Council's list of existing responsibilities. The development meant another increase in the Corporation's duty and power, but also, more importantly, a further improvement in the welfare of Southampton and its inhabitants.

UNWANTED IMPORTS FROM JERSEY AND GUERNSEY

The trade with the Channel Islands that over the years had been such a crucial mainstay of Southampton's economy brought with it another considerably less desirable factor. Criminals that had been convicted of crimes on the islands were at the time subject not to a specific set of regulated laws, but to the discretion of the individual courts dealing with their cases. Some of the offenders were 'transported to Southampton, Portsmouth, Weymouth and Plymouth and there let loose against the peace and security of the inhabitants of those places'. This worrying issue was brought to the attention of Southampton Corporation, and, in January 1840, a committee was appointed to investigate the possibility of imposing sanctions on 'the Captain or Master of any vessel ... landing or causing to be landed any person or persons convicted of felony in those Islands ... on the shores of Southampton'. The inquiries continued over some months and a former resident of Jersey, then living in Southampton (a Mr Abraham Jones Le Cras), informed the committee that a large percentage of felons had been transported to his new home town, especially those who would have become a burden to the island's poor relief. Le Cras revealed that he had recognised a number of Channel Island offenders in Southampton and the committee concluded that their presence would 'have a demoralising effect on the population'. An appeal was duly sent to the Home Office and a response was read to the Council in August 1840. The Home Secretary, Lord Normanby (who, rather incongruously, had earlier been a writer of romantic fiction), stood by the Islands' decisions to banish offenders not originating from those parts. However, he agreed with the Southampton Corporation that convicted islanders should not be deported to the mainland and resolved to 'take such steps as may appear necessary' were further cases to arise.

ten

THE SHIPPING COMPANIES

As the last memories of Southampton's spa days were consigned to history and with measures to deal with cholera in place, the transformation from tourist resort to thriving trading port was all but complete. In 1849, an anonymous writer observed: 'The town has assumed the busy look of a great commercial city, and one is astonished at the rapid change ... Bustle and activity prevail on all sides; ships landing and unloading on the quays; steamships and vessels of all sizes, arriving and departing; wagons, carts and trucks perambulating the streets.' The development of the docks had hastened the demise of the spa in one very specific way: the Royal Gloucester Baths was converted for use as the Dock Company's offices and was soon demolished to make way for an entirely new building. Similarly, the Long Rooms, once the epicentre of the town's social scene, were little used – more fashionable spa resorts, such as Cheltenham and Leamington, were now attracting the tourists who once holidayed in Southampton.

The census of 1851 recorded a population of 34,000, approximately a quarter higher than the previous census, in 1841. Most significantly, the vast majority of the increase took place in St Mary's ward, which saw a rise in population from 15,000 to 21,000. The fact that the bulk of the expansion was occurring in the working-class areas close to the docks and the Terminus station was yet another irrefutable indicator of the direction of Southampton's development.

In March 1851, the port welcomed the American frigate *St Lawrence*, which had sailed across the Atlantic bearing her country's contributions to the Great Exhibition; this began in London in May. Southampton's mayor invited the American President, Millard Fillmore to use the docks for the purpose, and extra incentive was given by offering a berth free of charge. The arrival of *St Lawrence* created nationwide interest, especially since her cargo contained a highly anticipated and revolutionary reaping machine designed by

The High Street, looking north towards the Bargate, mid-nineteenth century.

Above Bar Street, looking south towards the Bargate, mid-nineteenth century.

Cyrus McCormick. The following month the Turkish vessel *Feizi Baari* arrived at Southampton, also carrying items bound for the Great Exhibition.

At this time, the town was under the mayoralty of the remarkable Richard Andrews – a tenure of three consecutive years that had not been achieved for four centuries. Andrews had been born in rural Hampshire, the son of a wheelwright, and after a few years' schooling began to work at an early age. In 1821, he reputedly walked a distance of some 20 miles to reach Southampton, earning himself a later comparison with Dick Whittington in the process. Andrews found employment with one of the town's coachbuilders and only eleven years later, his experience and savings allowed him to set up his own company. He soon became the leading coach-maker in town, and perhaps nationally, supplying carriages to four Continents and being one of the few manufacturers in this trade to survive the downturn brought about by the expansion of the railways.

Andrews became a prominent figure in Southampton. He entered local politics with great enthusiasm and determination despite his rudimentary education. His background made him sympathetic with the anti-Corn Law movement, and Richard Cobden reportedly commented on Andrews's unlikely rise to political leadership: whereas in the North of England many men came from humble beginnings and progressed to prominence, such a path was almost unheard of in the south. Andrews worked tirelessly to promote the welfare of his adopted hometown, enhancing its reputation as a port.

Unafraid to display his allegiance to others whose causes he sympathised with, Andrews provided a grand reception for the Hungarian political exile Lajos Kossuth, who landed at Southampton in October 1851. Thousands thronged the High Street outside the Audit House and Kossuth was presented with the Hungarian Republic flag. Unfortunately, however, Andrews's life was not to end happily. In 1857, he promoted himself as a Liberal parliamentary candidate, but his defeat at the by-election that year devastated him, and he sank into depression and illness that culminated in his death two years later. A statue of Andrews was erected in 1860, and later East Park (where the statue stands) was renamed Andrews Park in his honour.

Meanwhile the port's trade continued to progress, thanks in no small part to the involvement of some other key individuals. A shipping company had been established in 1847 by US consul Joseph R. Croskey, who subsequently set up the New York and Havre Steam Navigation Company. Croskey's standing and contacts led to an agreement that the United States government would use his company's mail steamer service, which operated monthly sailings between

The memorial to Richard Andrews erected in East Park. Andrews was mayor five times, and, as a self-made man who had walked to the town from the countryside, became known as Southampton's Dick Whittington.

Southampton and New York. Meanwhile the two main companies using the port continued to be P&O and the Royal Mail, and the postal service expanded its operation in 1850, when it won the contract to deal with the mail routes to Brazil. A trial run was made at the end of 1850, but the service began officially in the summer of 1851. Facilities at the docks were further improved with the opening of the Inner (or Close) Dock in December 1851, at which a large crowd gathered to see a small steamer make her entrance. The new dock was connected to the Outer Dock, but was somewhat smaller, covering 10 acres and being 28ft deep; it was initially intended to handle shipments of coal and grain.

In addition to Croskey, another significant contributor to the development of the port was Joseph Stebbing, the man whose diplomacy had helped to implement public health improvements in Southampton. The son of an optician and manufacturer of nautical instruments, Stebbing moved to Southampton from Portsmouth in the 1830s and established his own business as an optician. His premises in Canute Road included a tower that was used as an observatory, its telescope offering excellent panoramic views of Southampton Water and the movements of vessels thereon. Stebbing soon became prominent, as both an entrepreneur and a politician, taking a leading role in the local Tory party, and particularly aware of the importance of railway and dock development. In 1851, he was a key contributor to the creation of the town's Chamber of Commerce and became its first president, serving in the role for a number of years.

Joseph Stebbing, a busy and prominent public figure, who among other interests was instrumental in founding Southampton's Chamber of Commerce.

The Southampton Chamber was formed largely as a response to an application made by its equivalent body in Liverpool that the northern port should take all the transatlantic mail service. As such, a policy would naturally have had an enormous negative impact on Southampton's trade, Stebbing and others were spurred into preventative action, 'to conduct the defence of the town's commercial rights and privileges and to promote its business interests'. Chambers of commerce in general was a relatively modern phenomenon – Southampton's was the eighth English branch – but their benefits were undeniable. The Chamber battled resolutely on behalf of the town and its businessmen, and in the coming years helped to assuage friction with both Liverpool and Plymouth.

The industrious Stebbing also found time to play an important part in the establishment of a new emigration company, which became more prominent in 1852 when Southampton was named as an official emigration port. The service, operated by the South Western Railway Company, was immediately extremely busy, with over 7,000 people departing for Australia over the following eight months.

However, not all the new companies that sprang up went on to flourish. In late 1852, the General Screw Steam Shipping Company was created, assisted once again by the endeavours of Joseph Croskey. As well as operating services to America, the firm hoped to run mail routes to India and the Cape of Good Hope, but its best intentions were ill founded and it was liquidated in 1856. That same year the future looked bright indeed for the European and Australian Steam Navigation Company, when it won a contract to operate the Australian mail route, but only two years later it too was in liquidation.

Despite these cautionary tales, in general the stories of success were more common than the failures. In January 1854, the world's largest ship, HMS *Himalaya*, departed from Southampton on her maiden voyage. The event created national interest and members of the public were able to tour the vessel before her sailing. In 1856, the Union Line formally made Southampton its base of operations, having been established in the town three years earlier as the Union Steam Collier Company. Its founders originally intended to transport coal to the port from South Wales, but the onset of the Crimean War, in 1853, had a considerable impact on this and many other shipping services, and a change of policy was enforced. In 1857, the company secured a five-year government contract to operate a monthly mail route to the Cape of Good Hope, and from the following year onwards, more destinations were added, among them St Helena and Mauritius. By this time, the Crimean War had drawn to a close. In its two-and-a-half-year duration, P&O steamers from Southampton had taken over 80,000 men and 15,000 horses to the battlefields of Crimea in the Black Sea region.

In 1857, vessels from Hamburg America Line began to use the port and the following year, the North German Lloyd Company (or Norddeutscher Lloyd) first called at Southampton en route between Bremen and New York. Joseph Croskey was again involved in this latter development, this time as the company's local agent. The theory has been put forward that the patronage of Southampton by these two companies was influential in later years, with the relocation of more passenger shipping services from the North of England to the south. In 1859, the South Western Railway Company considered withdrawing its emigration service to Australia, but once more the calming influence of Joseph Stebbing was brought to bear. In the event the route was maintained, and at a lower price to its users.

Three years later, the South Western Railway Company assumed control of steamship services to the Channel Islands, relocating operation from the Royal Pier to the docks. The Pier and Harbour Board (the members of which must have felt vindicated about their reservations over the new dock development)

The Red Funnel ferry terminal at Town Quay continued a long tradition of sailing to the Isle of Wight from Southampton.

was compensated for loss of earnings, but these payments were terminated early in the twentieth century. The Royal Pier remained in constant use, however. In 1861, two companies operating routes from the pier to the Isle of Wight merged to form the elaborately named Southampton, Isle of Wight and South of England Royal Mail Steam Packet Company, reputed to be the longest company name registered in the country. The newly amalgamated firm took control of a total of seven small ships, and appointed Andrew Lamb as its chairman, who boasted over two decades' experience as a superintendent with P&O. The following year, however, the Isle of Wight Company (as it had become known) further deflated the Pier and Harbour Board by moving its Southampton landing point away from the Royal Pier. Its new location was in the Chapel area of the town, situated on the western bank of the Itchen near the floating bridge, not necessarily a popular choice with most passengers. In 1865, another cross-Solent firm was merged into the greater whole, this time the similarly elaborately named Southampton, Isle of Wight and Portsmouth Improved Steamboat Company. The company boasted two small paddle vessels and more importantly the ownership of the landing pontoon at Cowes.

Southampton's Pier and Harbour Board evidently felt the financial loss of the move to Chapel keenly, and the next year similar landing facilities were constructed at the Royal Pier. Before long, the Isle of Wight service returned and remains there today.

～⌒◎ ◎⌒～

While developments continued on the seafront, other advances of a more cerebral nature were being made in the town with the foundation of the Hartley Institute. Henry Robinson Hartley had inherited a substantial fortune in 1800 upon the death of his father, also Henry – a successful wine merchant who had served as mayor in 1775. However, shortly after receiving his inheritance, Henry the younger left Southampton, and would never return there to live. Some speculated that he had 'taken aversion to the place', but whether this is true or not, Hartley visited 'so occasionally and privately that he was known by sight to few'. For at least some of the 1840s he lived in Newington in Surrey, and he died at the age of seventy-two in Calais, on 24 May 1850. It, therefore, came as a significant surprise that when Hartley's will was read it was discovered that he had left the vast majority of his wealth to Southampton Corporation. The value of the bequest amounted to over £100,000, intended to be used 'in such a manner as might best promote the study and advancement of the sciences of natural history, astronomy, antiquities, and classical and Oriental literature in the town of Southampton'. An institute was to be established in the Holy Rood district, in which Hartley's former home was situated, and originally even more facilities were mooted, including a public library, botanic gardens and an astronomical observatory.

Realising Hartley's intentions and ambitions, however, was not as easy as Southampton Corporation would have hoped .The will was challenged and a lengthy and costly legal battle ensued, taking eight years to resolve. By the time the wrangles were over, much of Hartley's original bequest was gone. Legal expenses accounted for £35,000 and once compromises had been reached with those contesting the will, less than £43,000 remained. In late 1858, the Council canvassed the opinions of the townspeople and plans were made to construct college buildings on the site of three High Street houses. One of the houses had been owned and used by Hartley's father and subsequently by Hartley himself, but it, along with the two neighbouring buildings, had fallen into disrepair and become 'a most melancholy eyesore'. Alternative locations were suggested, including the Marlands, on the basis that it would become a more central site owing to the expansion of the town in that direction. Ultimately it was this reasoning that secured the use of the High Street site, thanks in part, once again, to the contribution of Joseph Stebbing, who was prominently involved in the debates surrounding the bequest. The people of the area were keen to retain a substantial institution in this part of the town when others were moving further afield, and the choice meant that a historical link with Hartley's personal life was maintained.

The Hartley Institute was officially created in 1859, with £15,000 set aside for development of the site and construction of new buildings. Southampton Corporation donated some additional land at the rear of the site and building soon began. Lord Palmerston, the prime minister of the day, made the short journey from his Broadlands home in Romsey to lay the foundation stone on 8 January 1861. Onlookers must have hoped that the Hartley Institute would be blessed with a happier conclusion than the Polygon scheme, for which Palmerston's father had laid the foundation stone in 1768. In July 1862, Dr Francis Bond – 'a man of heroic stature' – was appointed to fulfil the combined roles of librarian and curator. Incredibly, the only other member of staff taken on at the time was a porter, although later a library and secretarial assistant joined Dr Bond.

Palmerston returned, on 15 October 1862, to perform the opening ceremony – an event that captured the imagination of the whole town. Some shops were closed, special trains were provided and the streets were decorated with flags, banners, and in some cases, illuminations. Palmerston was received on the Common by Mayor Frederick Perkins, members of the Corporation and many representatives of local bodies, and a military procession then made its way to the High Street. Inside the Hartley Institute's lecture hall the usual ceremonial speeches were given, followed by a sumptuous banquet and in the evening, a grand ball for over 500 people. The day produced, in the words of the *Hampshire Advertiser*'s report, a 'scene of general gaiety in the town' that would be unrivalled for many years to come.

Despite the celebrations, the Hartley Institute was not functional for nearly a year. The building work may have been completed but the necessary equipment was not yet in place: this part of the scheme had been delayed by the preparations for and expense of the lavish opening ceremony. Once finished, however, the Institute was an impressive sight, occupying a 74ft façade on the High Street and featuring a triple entrance. Inside, easily the largest room was the lecture theatre – 64ft long with galleries on either side and capable of

The main hall of the Hartley Institute, which was also used as a venue for concerts, balls and meetings.

accommodating around 1,000 people. Elsewhere there were libraries, a museum and a reading room, with the top floor occupied by the chemistry department. Finally, and presumably to the delight of Joseph Stebbing, an apartment was provided for the Chamber of Commerce. The Hartley Institute was overseen by a council that included the mayor and a number of other members of the town council, under whose guidance progress continued apace.

~⊚ ⊚~

While Southampton's educational stature was being enhanced, other more fundamental aspects demanded attention. Measures taken in response to the cholera outbreak of the late 1840s had proved inadequate and in some parts of the town conditions were once again repellent. As before, the poorer districts within the old town walls were most at risk: one area of only half a square mile was home to an incredible 3,200 people. Worse still, the streets closest to the shore were liable to flooding, often with sewage mixed into the sea water owing to blocked sewers. The most significant preventative step in combating these adversities was taken early in 1866, when James Lemon was appointed to the position of borough engineer.

Born on 15 January 1833 in Lambeth, the young James was educated privately in Westminster before entering a career in civil engineering. He spent seven years as an assistant to Sir Joseph Bazalgette, Chief Engineer of the Metropolitan Board of Works, who had been charged with overhauling London's foundering sewage system and whose engineering skills were so finely attuned that many miles of his great sewers are still in use today. Working with Bazalgette must have been invaluable experience for Lemon to bring to his role as Southampton's borough engineer. He was selected from sixty-two candidates on 10 January 1866 and held the post for the next twelve years. Under his direction, Southampton made great advances in terms of its sewerage and water supply, but Lemon later admitted that these undertakings were very nearly left to another man. A few months into his job he found the town's sanitary conditions so appalling – describing basements in Oxford Street that were 'flooded with sewage' – that he seriously considered resigning. To make matters worse, Lemon felt that his efforts were barely appreciated. 'Sanitarians were called panicmongers,' he noted ruefully, 'and the expenditure was considered an extravagant waste of money.'

The new cholera epidemic reached Southampton in the summer of 1866. As before, the worst affected areas were the low-lying, densely populated ones, but the number of deaths, while still significant, was less than in the previous outbreak. Despite this irrefutable validation of Lemon's concerns, he found it difficult to win allies in the Council. Even when faced with the rigours of cholera, the town councillors voted against providing an isolation hospital; instead they advocated incorporating such facilities into the new workhouse, which was being built on the site of the previous one close to St Mary's church. At the foundation-stone laying ceremony, the omnipresent Joseph Stebbing had, in keeping with the nature of the scheme, given a

James Lemon, the engineer who did so much to improve Southampton's sanitation, also served as mayor for two years.

speech in which he expounded on the moral value of thrift. These words, however, sounded somewhat less than convincing that very evening, when the day's attendees were invited to a celebratory mayor's feast at the Audit House, which featured a menu that the 500 potential new residents of the workhouse could only have dreamed about.

Lemon's wisdom was recognised in due course, however, when the Council reviewed his exhaustive assessment of the borough's sewerage system. Some of the engineer's ideas were successfully put into practice, although much of the northern region of the town was left until 1869 – when the Council was pressurised into action by a group of residents from the area. Two years later, concerns were also raised about the sanitary conditions in Portswood. Robert Morgan, a sanitary engineer, had written a report to the Local Government Board, which was heavily critical of the prevailing conditions, especially the proximity of sewage drains to the supplies of drinking water. Naturally, the board supported Morgan's findings and recommendations, and pressurised the Council to act on them, nevertheless, fierce debate on the subject ensued. On one hand, some councillors and those citizens living closer to the town centre objected to a large expenditure on such a small area. Conversely, the people of Portswood kept a rich sense of independence in their community, and disliked 'unwarrantable interference'. Eventually a compromise was reached, and the Council obtained a piece of land at St Denys on which James Lemon built a new sewage works. The benefits of the facility were soon evident, clearly seen in the improvement in conditions in Portswood, and before long, the lower part of Southampton was served by a new water main, consigning old wells to the past.

In 1877, Lemon also became involved in an issue that would take many years to resolve – the need for a new town hall. From the 1850s onwards, there had been a great increase in the number of new municipal offices constructed in Britain: more government legislation meant that more administrative staff were required, all of whom had to be accommodated. In some cases, the rivalry between towns (Leeds and Bradford, for example) produced a competitive desire to build a more impressive town hall and thus outdo the neighbouring town. In Southampton, the issue had arisen in 1874, when the Audit House was described as 'totally inadequate for the proper discharge of municipal business', but at a council meeting in August the plans were defeated, on the grounds of expense and a lack of public demand for the scheme.

Two and a half years later, in the spring of 1877, the Corporation was given the opportunity to purchase a 1½-acre property on Above Bar formerly owned by a Miss Ogle (the area through which Ogle Road now runs). The current municipal offices were again described as 'a disgrace to the town' and new buildings were envisaged on the Ogle site. Eventually it was decided to renovate or replace the Audit House on the existing site, and the chance to obtain the Ogle estate was lost – validation of Mayor Abraham's criticism of the more elderly members of the Council who 'did not seem to want anything new'. Lemon was equally scathing in his assessment, calling this 'one of the greatest blunders the Corporation ever made' when writing his *Reminiscences of Public Life In Southampton* in 1911.

By 1878, the sanitary enhancements to the town were being widely recognised. In March, the Whitehall Review enthused that 'there are few cleaner towns in England than Southampton' and that 'its bright appearance is decidedly wonderful'. That same year, however, James Lemon left his position as borough engineer to begin a private practice. His departure also allowed him to display an open political allegiance to the Liberal Party, which he had been unable to do while in the employ of the Corporation. Lemon's involvement in the town hall debate remained and he served the Corporation as a private consultant, continuing the work he had started as borough engineer. In early 1879, his plans for renovations to the Audit House were presented and a raucous public meeting was held at the Bargate, lasting over four hours.

Opposition to the scheme was widespread, but when Lemon managed to reduce the cost to £3,000 agreement was finally reached. Mayor J. Blount Thomas laid the foundation stone of the new works in October 1879, although the *Southampton Times* predicted that the scheme would become 'a perpetual memorial of municipal folly in Southampton'. A year later, the renovated Audit House was reopened, accompanied by the obligatory celebratory dinner with lavish foods and wines. Lemon and the builder, J. Crook, were both praised for their efforts and although the former declared himself satisfied with the scheme that day, he still felt compelled to ask in his memoirs, 'When shall we see a new Town Hall? I fear not in my lifetime.' This turned out to be an astute prediction: despite the subject's emergence a number of times, it would not be resolved for another fifty years.

MAJOR-GENERAL CHARLES GORDON

One man who bore witness to the rapid changes and progress taking place in Victorian Southampton was none other than Major-General Charles George Gordon, who would go on to be immortalised for his involvement (and death) in Britain's imperial conflicts. Gordon's parents lived at No.5 Rockstone Place, one of the grand Regency residences built in the town that reflected the prosperous spa resort years, and would later be so widely admired. The Gordons lived at the house throughout the 1860s and Charles visited regularly, staying at the property when on leave from his duties during the British occupation of northern China and subsequent operations in that country. In the early 1870s, Gordon moved on to Africa, but, in 1874, he purchased No.5 Rockstone Place after the death of his parents, and his sisters continued to live there for over forty years. The general himself, however, would not achieve such longevity: he was killed in Khartoum in January 1885 in circumstances that are still not entirely clear. In death, he was celebrated as an imperial hero and memorials to him were swiftly erected all over the world, from London to Melbourne in Australia. In October 1885, only nine months after his death, a monument to General Gordon was unveiled in Queen's Park in Southampton, close to Town Quay and overlooked by the South Western Hotel. A solid, imposing construction capped with a crucifix, it serves as a permanent reminder of Gordon's association with the town.

Above General Gordon's family home in Rockstone Place, 2011.

Right The memorial to Major-General Charles Gordon, 2011.

eleven

EXPANSION OF
THE TOWN & DOCKS

During the 1870s, while Southampton Corporation focused on sanitation and its municipal buildings, trade in the port continued in stable if unspectacular fashion. The opening of the Suez Canal in 1869 naturally enhanced commerce with the east, particularly for P&O, and business with South Africa was also healthy. However, this progress combined with the technological advances of the day did not entirely act in the port's favour. Not only was the volume of shipping increasing but the size of the vessels was also growing, as commerce demanded larger cargoes transported at faster speeds. Inevitably, the quayside facilities at Southampton docks started to become inadequate: more berths were required with deeper water, as well as greater storage facilities.

By 1874, P&O was so dissatisfied with the conditions that it threatened to relocate its base of operations to London – a threat that was partially carried out the next year with the removal of the company's cargo services. Even worse, many employees also made the move to the capital, which made an impact on other aspects of the local economy. Attempting to rectify the situation, the Dock Company tried to raise the finances to build a new dock, issuing appeals to the South Western Railway Company and Southampton Corporation itself. However, these efforts were in vain and ultimately P&O ran out of patience and relocated to London entirely, in 1881. The news came as a significant blow to the town and port, and many feared that other companies, possibly including the Royal Mail, would also depart.

With such uncertainty in the air, it was, perhaps, not the most opportune time for an extension to be added to one of Southampton's most prestigious hotels. The South Western Hotel (originally called the Imperial) opened adjacent to the Terminus station in 1867, elaborately designed in a French Renaissance style by architect John Norton. It changed its name a few years later upon being taken over by the railway company, and, in 1882, was extended on its northern

After a long and varied life, South Western House is still an impressive sight.

side, closest to the station. Despite the troubled times, the hotel survived and, indeed, prospered; its opulence and proximity to the docks made it a desirable stopping point for many of the port's wealthier passengers in the years to come.

Two years later, work on another important building was completed; this time of spiritual rather than commercial value. St Mary's church, often known as the 'mother church' of Southampton, had occupied a number of buildings on or near the same spot since the visit of St Birinus in the seventh century. The fourth church on the site was constructed in the early eighteenth century, but later alterations were clumsily carried out and the long-term future of the structure appeared to be in jeopardy. Indeed, in the early 1870s, the Bishop of Winchester, Samuel Wilberforce (who had become well known for railing against the new evolutionary theories of Charles Darwin) consulted with the architect, George Street, who saw no value in retaining the building. Street's reputation had been enhanced by his successful design for the Royal Courts of Justice in London, which Southampton firm Bull & Sons began building in 1873. Sadly, Wilberforce died the same year, and it was not until 1878 that work on Street's design for the new church was properly under way. That August, the Prince of Wales (who went on to be King Edward VII) laid the dedication stone and the building was consecrated in June the following year. Construction finally drew to a close in 1884, although George Street did not live to see his plans completed. Even when the rest of the church was finished, the tower and spire remained unbuilt for a further thirty years.

Above The ceremony laying the foundation stone for the rebuilt St Mary's church, in 1878.

Right St Mary's church, 2011.

With the town hall issue at least temporarily assuaged, meanwhile, James Lemon returned his attention to his first area of expertise – Southampton's sanitary arrangements. Deciding to devote himself to further improving the town's water supply, he entered the Council in 1883 to campaign on the issue. In the Victorian period, the town's population had grown from under 28,000 in 1841 to over 65,000 in 1891; this increase overburdened the supply from the surface reservoirs on the Common that a century earlier had proved adequate. Indeed, in the intervening years a number of attempts were made to source a more plentiful supply from the Common, but with little success. Between July 1838 and February 1851 extensive excavations were made with the intention of sinking an artesian well, but after thirteen years the project was abandoned – 'the results not being considered sufficiently promising', despite boring to a depth of over 1,000ft at a cost of around £20,000.

Following these frustrations, the Corporation contemplated two possibilities for a new water supply, either from Otterbourne or Mansbridge. The Mansbridge option was taken up first, but owing to 'the unsatisfactory and indeed potentially unhealthy condition of this water', James Lemon's enthusiasm for an alternative was ignited. Thanks to his campaigning, the waterworks at Otterbourne was opened in 1888. A greatly improved supply was provided and much of Southampton's water is still sourced from the area today.

Further positive news was soon in store with developments in the expansion of the docks. Fears that the relocation of P&O to London would herald the beginning of a larger exodus had not been realised, and the port had steadily and surely survived. Plans were proposed to extend the Itchen Quay by nearly 2,000ft, while Alfred Giles proffered a scheme including nearly twice as much new quay as well as a 16-acre dock. The Corporation formulated a plan to raise £200,000 for the work through a parliamentary bill, which it would then provide to the Dock Company as a loan, but the trepidation of the company's shareholders prevented the progress of the scheme. Finally, in 1886, the Dock Company secured financing of £250,000 from the South Western Railway Company, which facilitated the building of a third dock. After three years of construction, the work was complete. The dock was the first in the country that allowed even the largest vessels to come and go whatever the position of the tide – a huge benefit to the disparate shipping companies that used the port. In July 1890, Queen Victoria visited the town to perform the opening ceremony of the new Empress Dock – its name recognising the superfluous title awarded to her by Disraeli in 1876.

The day was the most spectacular and colourful seen in the town since the opening of the Hartley Institute nearly thirty years earlier. Members of the Corporation assembled at the Audit House before midday and made their way in procession to the Terminus station to board a special train that took them the short distance to the docks. On arrival, they retired to 'an elaborately decorated and spacious shed' overlooking the quay, at which the royal yacht would arrive later. Soon afterwards, they were joined by Steuart MacNaghten (Chairman of the Dock Company) and other board members, and at about 1.30 p.m. another special train arrived from Waterloo station, which had superseded Nine Elms as the London terminus of the Southampton line in 1848. This brought more distinguished guests on a train entirely made up of brand new carriages, which came to a halt in the luncheon shed itself, such that 'the unusual spectacle was witnessed of a train in a dining room'. Edward Benson, the Archbishop of Canterbury, said grace and a magnificent lunch was served.

A great number of toasts and speeches followed, including one by Alfred Giles, the chairman of the Union Steamship Company and one of the town's MPs. Alfred was the son of Francis Giles, whose work on the London–Southampton railway had ended somewhat ignominiously, but had also been the engineer for the first phase of the new docks as inaugurated in 1838. Alfred had followed in his father's professional footsteps and became consulting engineer to the Southampton Dock Company. His speech gave some technical details about the new dock and he expressed his bafflement that some shipping companies still preferred to use London rather than Southampton. After a toast offered by Mayor Bishop, the assembly adjourned to the quayside to await the arrival of the queen.

Around the quayside, a crowd estimated at between 25,000 and 30,000 people had been gathering for three hours, with admission to the areas closest to the queen's arrival gained by a colour-coded ticketing system. Some daring observers ventured onto roofs to improve their vantage points: 'Every available spot, from which anything like a glimpse could be obtained, was crowded,' in the words of the *Southampton Times*. At 4.20 p.m., the royal yacht, *Alberta*, made her way up Southampton Water and approached the new dock, as church bells in the town rang out in accompaniment. The yacht entered the dock, breaking a ceremonial ribbon in the process and the crowds saw the queen properly for the first time, serenely seated in an armchair on the deck. As a band played the national anthem, she acknowledged the cheering onlookers.

A reception party then boarded the yacht and Steuart MacNaghten gave an address of welcome, to which the queen replied:

> It gives me great satisfaction to inaugurate this important addition to the Docks of the Port of Southampton and to see so striking an illustration of the energy of commercial enterprise in my kingdom. I trust that the Port of Southampton will feel the benefit of the great work you have completed and will exhibit in the future increasing developments of trade and prosperity.

After several more speeches, including a further response from the queen, the ceremonial duties were complete. At nearly 5.30 p.m., just over an hour since the cutting of the ribbon to open the new dock, the royal yacht headed back into Southampton Water for the return journey to Cowes. The queen had performed the opening ceremony without even setting foot on the quayside and arrived back on the Isle of Wight at 7.00 p.m. to retire to Osborne House.

In Southampton, meanwhile, the celebrations continued. A reception was held at the Audit House for Corporation members and guests, and at the quayside 'luncheon shed' there was a supper for Dock Company employees and the workmen who had constructed the new dock. At the same time, the Dock Company chairman, Steuart MacNaghten was hosting a party at his Bitterne Manor House home. As the historic day drew to a close, the townspeople must have hoped that MacNaghten's wish 'that this enlargement of Southampton's Docks may be productive of great benefit not only to the Port of Southampton but also to the trade and commerce of the country generally' would come to pass.

MacNaghten's optimism, however, was soon undermined by industrial action that brought an entirely different atmosphere to the docks. Within weeks of the great celebrations, Southampton dockers created their own union to campaign for improved working conditions, inspired by their London counterparts, who the previous year had successfully achieved a landmark pay increase to 6*d* an hour. With other such actions proving fruitful in both Portsmouth and Plymouth, Southampton's dock workers elected to strike, requesting pay rises, reduced working hours and acknowledgement of their new union. They received some encouragement from Canon Scannell, the popular priest from St Joseph's Roman Catholic church in Bugle Street. Scannell was a well-known and well-respected figure to the dockers and he served as an intermediate in the negotiations, securing an offer of increased pay.

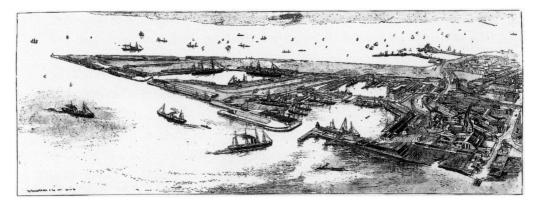
An aerial view of the docks, late nineteenth century.

Despite the priest's efforts, the shipping companies refused to recognise the new trade union, and, suitably affronted, the workers began their strike at midnight on 7 September 1890. A crowd of men gathered in Canute Road, thwarting anyone's attempts to enter the docks and stopping trains going in and coming out. Two days later, 'all work in the docks was brought to a stand-still', local and county police charged at the assembled throngs with little or no success, and military reinforcements were drafted in from Portsmouth. Less than two months after reading an address of welcome to Queen Victoria, one of the greatest days in his town's history, Mayor James Bishop found himself reading the Riot Act to a mass of striking dockers. The troops had some limited success, but they and the mayor were soon pelted with stones. Despite exhortations that he should order the troops to open fire, Bishop instead deployed the fire brigade, who used hoses to clear enough of Canute Road to allow the soldiers to reclaim it.

The sodden strikers retaliated on something of a personal level by making haste to Bishop's shop in East Street, which they partially demolished. Those hoping to achieve a similar result at the mayor's house in Grosvenor Square were confronted with a guard of troops, but Bishop felt the need for further reinforcements at the docks and more arrived shortly afterwards. While a torpedo boat and gunboats patrolled the waters around the docks, it was made clear to the strikers that the man in charge of the troops, Colonel White, would be less reticent about opening fire than Mayor Bishop had been. This served to defuse the situation, and finally an agreement was reached. In the aftermath, a number of the main protagonists were given prison sentences, while others were fined. Mayor Bishop's future was also affected by the strike: the stresses and strains of the incident caused him to suffer from 'congestion of the brain'. His recovery took several months, after which he elected to leave some bad memories behind him and relocated to Portsmouth, moving his shoe shop business with him.

⁂

It was not long before the opening of the Empress Dock was no longer the most important day in the history of the port. In a way, the new dock only served to emphasise the inadequacies of the older facilities, and it quickly became clear that further developments were necessary. Once again, the Dock Company did not possess the finances needed for the work, and was actually having difficulty keeping up with loan repayments to the South Western Railway Company. Perhaps inevitably, the sale of the company was mooted. Negotiations ensued, and, in October 1892, the docks were sold to the South Western Railway Company for nearly £1.4m. This sale enabled further investment, including the dredging of Southampton Water and the construction of new quays, allowing vessels of ever-increasing size to use the docks. As the number of ports able to accommodate large ships reduced, Southampton's commercial position was strengthened and in time its future would be assured.

The sale of the docks took place in the mayoralty of James Lemon, who reached the peak of his council service when he was elected to the role on November 1891. During his two-year tenure, work also began on a new library at the southern end of Bedford Place, and Lemon himself laid the foundation stone at the end of August 1892. Around the country increasing numbers of libraries were opening, thanks to the Public Libraries Act of 1850 and growing literacy levels. Libraries in Southampton had enjoyed something of a mixed history, beginning with the coffee houses and reading rooms that became popular during the town's years as a spa resort. The Corporation's library, meanwhile, for many years consisted largely of a collection of books donated by George Pitt in 1831. Little is known about Pitt – he was described as a merchant from French Street, and (either additionally or alternatively) a military captain. His book collection, while undoubtedly valuable, was equally obscure. Many of the titles dated from the early eighteenth century and ranged from academic text books to history and science. Most notably, none of the collection was printed in English. On the opening of the Hartley Institute, in 1862, Pitt's books were passed to the reference library, where they may at least have found a greater degree of appreciation.

Southampton's first public library did not open until 1889, following pressure from the Hartley Institute and the town's Parliamentary Debating Society, a body which as much as anything else provided a forum for prospective town councillors to test out their skills of oratory. A public meeting confirmed the decision, and the library was opened in two upper rooms above stables in St Mary's Street, previously the location of a music hall. But not all residents appreciated the new facility: on some occasions the chief librarian had to be escorted home by a policeman since a few of the locals 'thought it amusing to treat the library as a joke and to manhandle the staff'. Despite this, the construction of a new library provoked a heated debate, with some people even opposing the relocation.

By the time of the opening, nearly a year after the laying of the foundation stone in July 1893, the new building was described as one 'admirably suited to the purpose it is designed to fulfil'. The opening ceremony was performed by Dr Kitchin, the Dean of Winchester, who had previously lectured at the Hartley Institute. The architect, A.E.J. Guy of Southsea, had provided a handsome, red-brick building with a central tower into which the main entrance was set. The entrance hall housed a memorial bust of the late Timothy Falvey, a prominent and popular local figure who was widely respected in Southampton. He had been the editor of the *Hampshire Independent* newspaper and was involved, alongside Lemon, in the debates over a new town hall. Inside there were three main areas: the reading room, the newsroom and the lending library, with additional staff accommodation on the first floor. Previous doubts about the choice of site were put aside and the quality of the new facilities was roundly praised.

The same year more progress was made in Southampton's port trade. Dredging, which had begun the previous decade, increased the depth of the approach channels to 30ft to accommodate the increasingly large vessels in operation. The benefits of the sale of the docks to the railway company also continued, most notably in the form of a new agreement with the American Line shipping company. The Pennsylvania-based firm had itself increased dramatically in size a few years earlier when it took over the Inman Line, which had originally transported immigrants. Having primarily used Liverpool as its British base of operations, in 1893 the American Line elected to transfer its services to Southampton. The occasion was commemorated on Saturday, 4 March with the ceremonial arrival of the line's ship, *New York*. The American flag was flown at both the Audit House and the Bargate, the docks were opened to the public, and church bells rang out across the town.

Mayor James Lemon and his Corporation colleagues spent the afternoon aboard a steamer, which sailed out to meet *New York* near Hurst Castle. As the two ships headed towards the docks, Lemon was struck with fear when he noticed that the tide was exceptionally low. 'One of two things is going to happen,' he later recalled. 'Either this port is going to be made today, or it is going to be damned forever. If the American ship gets aground she will not come here again.' Mercifully, the ship made the approach successfully and arrived safely at the Empress Dock to the rejoicing of the assembled crowds. London-bound passengers who disembarked were transferred to a special train called *American Eagle*, the luxurious carriages having been built in Eastleigh. *New York* remained in the port for a week, during which time there was great rejoicing in the town. More than 3,000 people toured the ship during her stay, with the admission fees donated to charity. The agreement with the American Line further enhanced the financial surety of the docks, which manifested in more new developments. Also in 1893, cranes on Town Quay were converted for use with electricity, the first such cranes in Britain to be powered in this way. By 1895, the Railway Company had spent over £2m, including the completion that year of the Prince of Wales dry dock, which was opened by the future King Edward VII in August. At 750ft long it was the largest of its kind in the world, an indication of the advances in shipbuilding that saw the launching of bigger and bigger vessels.

As the docks and the ships they accommodated expanded, so too did Southampton itself. A council committee was created to investigate the possibility of extending the borough boundaries, including in its number James Lemon. In 1894, the town's borough engineer had submitted a report in which he warned that the land available for building would be exhausted within two years, and that the population of around 70,000 people constituted a comparatively small borough. As well as the extra space that would be gained by extending the boundaries, there were other obvious advantages to the plan. The district of Shirley in particular was a prime area for inclusion, suffering as it did from an inadequate sewerage system and the lack of a hospital. Furthermore, the absence of a police authority had led to the creation of an independent body known as the Garden Protection Society.

Nevertheless, both Shirley and Freemantle opposed the boundary extension, and the stalemate resulted in an enquiry by an inspector from the Local Government Board – Major-General C. Phipps Carey. The investigation began in January 1895 in the Hartley Institute's lecture hall, with testimony provided by a great many people, including former Dock Company chairman, Sir Steuart MacNaghten and representatives from Southampton Corporation, the South Hants Water Company and the Itchen Floating Bridge Company. Ultimately, the wishes of the borough council were fulfilled: the Board concluded that Shirley, Freemantle, South Stoneham, the Bitterne Park estate and part of Millbrook should be incorporated, and the associated Act of Parliament was ratified in August that year. James Lemon observed that the inhabitants of those areas 'belonged by feeling, by sentiment, by unity to Southampton, and they ought to be in the Borough'.

Although the town had now significantly increased in size, the Corporation focused on the redevelopment of one of its oldest districts, within the town walls. As well as the borough engineer's report of 1894, which helped to pave the way for the extension of the borough boundary, the same year also saw an investigation by the borough medical officer of health into conditions in the town's slums. The Simnel Street area was of particular concern, and had a reputation to match its environment: respectable townsfolk seldom visited and there were notorious fights on Saturday nights. The street was narrow and dark, with timber beams bracing opposing buildings against each other to prevent collapse. Most alarmingly, the density of population in the district was nearly 450 people per acre, over thirty times higher than that in Portswood. The improvement plan taken up in 1895 cleared many of the dank and dirty alleys and lanes in the area and provided new artisans' dwellings. A clean, modern lodging house in St Michael's Square was completed four years later.

Having quite literally enlarged the boundaries of its responsibility, the Corporation also sought to extend its ownership of the services it provided. In 1896, it purchased the Electric Light and Power Company for £21,000, thus taking control of the town's electricity supply. The company had previously operated a generating station at the Back of the Walls, and soon its new owners spent nearly £30,000 upgrading this station and extending the mains supply in the town. Southampton's Tramways Company was bought out in 1898, and the Corporation proceeded to modernise and expand the service. These developments were overseen by Frederick Dunsford, who was appointed chairman of the Council's tramways committee after the completion of the purchase. Dunsford, who owned a drapery shop in the town, would hold the position for over twenty-four years, becoming known as 'The Tramways King'. Before long, the Corporation's two recent purchases benefited each other with the electrification of the tramways.

The people of Southampton, both old and new, may have been impressed and reassured by the Corporation's enthusiasm for improving public services, but soon they found themselves living in a town heavily involved in military operations. In October 1899, the Second Boer War broke out and Southampton, having been designated Britain's premier military port five years earlier, was thrown into frantic action. The conflict served to illustrate the capabilities of the docks, as James Lemon observed, 'the close connection by rail from Aldershot to the ship's side was so advantageous that the troops were constantly embarked without a hitch of any kind'.

In April 1900, the town welcomed General Sir George White upon his return to Britain, following his role as commander of the forces at the famous Siege of Ladysmith. Already the recipient of the Victoria Cross for his earlier heroics in Afghanistan, White was greeted by Mayor George Hussey, members of the Corporation, and, naturally, his wife and their daughter. A large crowd enthusiastically cheered his return and after the singing of the national anthem, White and his family and friends travelled to London by train. At times the scenes in and around the docks must have been truly remarkable. A month before General White's arrival, 11,000 men had left the port in just six days and over the three years that the war lasted, the vast majority of the vessels heading for South Africa left from Southampton. More than half a million troops departed and arrived at the port, along with many tons of weapons and other equipment. Compared with events in the coming decades, however, the burden of the Boer War on Southampton's docks would pale into insignificance.

JOHN EVERETT MILLAIS

While Southampton's industrial and economic development progressed, one of the town's sons was enjoying a successful career in more artistic circles. John Everett Millais was born in the town in 1829 and his talents were recognised before he had even reached his teens: he was accepted at the Royal Academy schools aged only eleven. In 1848, Millais became one of the founding members of the Pre-Raphaelite Brotherhood, alongside William Holman Hunt and Dante Gabriel Rossetti. As a group, they rebelled against some of the classical doctrines of art, earning themselves a reputation in the eyes of some as the first avant-garde movement. Indeed, two years later, Millais courted further controversy with his work *Christ In The House Of His Parents*, which depicted Jesus and his family living in less than salubrious conditions and was a marked departure from the august tone of previous such portrayals. One of the painting's most prominent critics was none other than Charles Dickens, who objected to almost every element of the work, and the furore led Queen Victoria to ask to view it at Buckingham Palace. Although some of Millais's subsequent works were also controversial, none incited a reaction as hostile, and thereafter his paintings gradually tended more towards the mainstream art of the time, showing an appreciation of the seventeenth-century masters. However, his change of style was attacked by critics such as John Ruskin and William Morris, with the latter accusing Millais of yielding to the fashions of the day in order to sell more of his works. In his later years, Millais painted a number of landscapes in Scotland, many of which are now highly regarded, and, in 1896, he was elected President of the Royal Academy. Sadly, Millais's tenure in the role was short-lived, as he died that same year, and was buried in St Paul's Cathedral. In recent years, Millais's legacy has been commemorated in his place of birth, with the naming of the Millais Gallery in East Park Terrace, part of Solent University.

twelve

RMS *TITANIC*
& THE FIRST WORLD WAR

The end of the Boer War brought with it a brief downturn in the shipping industry and the port's trade in general, but the ensuing recovery led to even greater progress as the new century dawned. In 1905, the Trafalgar Dry Dock was completed after four years of construction. The dock was named in honour of the centenary of the famous naval battle, and surpassed even the Prince of Wales Dock in its magnitude at nearly 1,000ft long and 100ft wide. It was opened by the Lord Lieutenant of Hampshire, Henry Paulet, on the date of the great battle in October and was first used the following month. Two years later, further dredging of the approach to the port added an extra 2ft to the depth of the channel.

The undertaking of such facilities and enhancements was prescient, as also in 1907 the White Star Line relocated its North Atlantic service from Liverpool to Southampton. The company had originally been formed in Liverpool, specialising in routes to Australia. It later expanded its services, but by the first decade of the twentieth century, it faced increasingly stiff competition from Cunard Line ships, such as the *Lusitania* and *Mauretania*, both of which mostly operated services from Liverpool to New York. Its first ship to arrive in Southampton was the *Adriatic*; she was almost brand new, having undertaken her maiden voyage from Liverpool in May 1907. Transferred to Southampton immediately after her maiden voyage, she entered the docks the same month, greeted by council representatives on board a paddle steamer that accompanied her to her berth. White Star's first vessel to leave the port bound for New York was *Celtic*, also departing in May.

In a further effort to compete with Cunard, the White Star Line announced, in 1907, that it would build three new vessels: the 'Olympic Class' ships would surpass Cunard's finest in both scale and luxury. Construction of the first liner was to begin in late 1908, by which time the builders, Harland & Wolff of Belfast, had also established their own engineering facilities in Southampton alongside the Trafalgar Dry Dock. The *Olympic* was launched in October 1910 and, with what would turn out to be somewhat ominous luck, was almost immediately damaged in a collision with the quayside and, therefore, had to undergo repairs before being fitted out. Early in June the following year, she arrived in Southampton as the world's largest ship and was housed in the newly constructed White Star Dock, a 15-acre deep-water berth that would be used by all three of the sister ships. The *Olympic* departed for New York on her maiden voyage later that month, under the command of Captain Edward Smith. Three months later, with Smith at the helm once again, the *Olympic* was leaving Southampton Water on her fifth journey to the United States when she collided with the cruiser, HMS *Hawke*. The pride of the White Star Line was seriously damaged, with a large hole torn in the side of her hull that would take more than two months to repair. More difficult to address was the damage to the company, both in terms of reputation and finance: the accident was estimated to have cost £250,000 in repairs and lost revenue. The owners of the line must have hoped that the next sister ship, being fitted out in Belfast at the time, would be blessed with better fortune.

❧ ❦

The largest ship ever made was not the only world-famous attraction to be seen in Southampton in 1911. Harry Houdini, the great magician and escapologist, had already visited the town over a decade earlier when he first arrived in Britain after a voyage on the American Line vessel, SS *Kensington*. In the spring of 1911, Houdini returned to Southampton to begin a week of shows at the Hippodrome Theatre in Ogle Road. By now his reputation preceded him and he performed twice nightly for the length of his residency, which began on Monday, 24 April. Houdini's act at the time included an escape from a padlocked milk churn filled with water, as well as freeing himself from a straitjacket and various other restraints. These feats were evidently of great interest to the Associated Wizards of the South, to whom Houdini was introduced at their meeting during his week in the town. Harry graciously donated a portrait of himself to each member and contributed an article for their monthly newsletter. In return, he was made an honorary member of the society.

On Saturday, 29 April, Houdini's last day at the Hippodrome, he performed a new escape that any of the Associated Wizards of the South would have been thrilled and astounded by, if only they had been there to witness it. Houdini's Saturday matinée, according to popular legend, was attended by an audience of just one. The extra show was not advertised in either the *Southampton Times* or the *Hampshire Advertiser*, and the cost of admission was raised to the inordinate sum of 1 guinea. If the matinée was indeed seen by a solitary viewer, that lucky audience member was given a private first performance of an escape with which Houdini enthralled crowds all over the world for years to come. The Water Torture Cell was a large cabinet made of mahogany with a glass front panel and filled with water. In the lid of the cabinet were two holes that served as stocks: Houdini's feet were inserted into the holes and firmly fastened. Once secure, the lid was raised up above the stage on a pulley, so that he hung upside down by his ankles. He was then lowered into the cabinet, head first, and entirely submerged in the water, whereupon the lid was locked in place by his stage assistants. A curtain was drawn around the cabinet and the orchestra began its musical accompaniment. Less than a minute later, the curtain was thrown aside and Houdini stood before his audience – breathless and dripping wet, but free of all restraints.

Houdini did not reprise the Water Torture Cell escape in his evening performance at the Hippodrome, and that night the cabinet was taken to London where it remained in storage for over a year – the Upside Down, as it also became known, did not reappear until the autumn of 1912. He was evidently delighted with the illusion, describing it in a letter as 'the greatest spectacular thing ever witnessed on the stage', and the escape became such an integral part of his act that it remained in his repertoire almost up until his death, in 1926. Few, if any, of the thousands of people who saw Harry escape from the water-filled cabinet over the years would have known that it was first attempted before an audience of one on a spring Saturday afternoon in Southampton.

⚜

By the spring of the following year, 1912, the *Olympic*'s sister ship was complete and almost ready to enter service. In early April, *Titanic* was given a brief sea trial and arrived in Southampton on the morning of 4 April. Unlike her sister, the new vessel was not opened for public tours before her maiden voyage, either at Liverpool or Southampton. *Titanic* left less than a week later, on 10 April, and was involved in a dramatic incident before she had even left Southampton Water. As *Titanic* pulled away from her berth, the wake created caused another vessel docked alongside her to break its moorings, and this vessel was drawn towards the large liner; collision was avoided by just a few feet. The second ship

Sister ships *Olympic* and *Titanic* side by side during the building process. (Library of Congress, LC-USZ62-67359)

Titanic departing from Southampton in April 1912, never to return.

was none other than the *New York*, which had entered Southampton with great ceremony in 1893 to herald the arrival of the American Line.

The near miss did not augur well. Five days later *Titanic* sank to the bottom of the Atlantic after striking an iceberg, with the loss of over 1,500 souls – at the time, the greatest disaster in maritime history. When the news first reached Southampton the following day, however, little certainty could be attached to any of the details. An ambiguous notice was posted at the offices of the *Southampton Times*, which was enough to spread panic and disbelief through-out the town; in Canute Road, many congregated around the White Star Line offices waiting for further news. The Bargate's borough flag was flown at half mast while in Northam – the area from which a large number of the ship's crew came – relatives were also fearing the worst. The Girls' School log for 15 April recorded: 'A great many girls are absent this afternoon owing to the sad news regarding the *Titanic*. Fathers and brothers are on the vessel; and some of the little ones have been in tears all afternoon.' Two days later, the survivors' lists began to appear, although they contained inaccuracies that cruelly brought unwarranted grief to some and false hope to others. As the picture became clearer over the coming days, so the sense of loss increased – not only on a per-sonal level for the bereaved, but also because the port's greatest attraction, the largest and most luxurious ship in the world, was never to return. 'The gloom which hangs over Southampton is intensified daily,' observed the *Daily Mirror*, 'and the agonizing scenes at the docks could move the hardest hearts to compassion.'

On 20 April, a memorial service took place at St Mary's church, and eight days later a much larger open-air service was held on the Marlands. A relief fund was set up in order to assist widows and orphans left behind by the trag-edy, raising money through charity events such as concerts at the Hippodrome and Palace theatres, street collections and the sale of commemorative post-cards. The total collected came to over £400,000, but, of course, nothing could compensate the people of Southampton in their time of grief. Around 600 homes in Southampton were directly affected by the disaster, and over 100 children at Northam School lost a parent or relative on the ship. The town had not been dealt such a crushing blow since the French raid nearly 600 years ear-lier. The loss of *Titanic* – 'a floating emblem of the Edwardian class structure' in the words of historian A.N. Wilson – was a stark reminder that Britain's seem-ingly inexorable industrial progress and taming of the elements could be torn apart just as ice could tear through steel.

As the town was still coming to terms with the tragedy, the issue of new municipal buildings (including a town hall) came to the fore once more. The subject had surfaced a number of times since James Lemon had overseen renovations to the Audit House in 1880, but little progress had been made. One potential location regularly suggested was the Hartley Institute in the High Street. The Hartley had been recognised as a university in 1902, thirteen years after its first application for the status, but, by 1913, it was widely acknowledged that time had caught up with the buildings and they were not to fulfil a useful purpose for much longer. Plans for their adaptation to municipal purposes, however, were never fulfilled.

The key activist in the latest campaign was Sidney Kimber, whose father Richard had been the headmaster of St Mary's School and later founded a brickworks in Highfield. Sidney worked at his father's company and at a young age joined Portswood Conservative Association and the Parliamentary Debating Society. He was attracted to the latter by the fact that one of its resolutions had played a significant part in the construction of the new library inaugurated by James Lemon in 1892; indeed, the building had been made with Kimber bricks. Kimber had first become a town councillor in 1910, and remained a prominent public figure almost until his death nearly forty years later. Dismissing the Hartley as a viable site, Kimber instead preferred the use of the Marlands – part of the town's public land that had previously been home to a leper hospital and was on occasion used as a drill ground. Discussions took place in the summer of 1914 and even Britain's declaration of war, on 4 August, did not initially deter Kimber from his cause: 'If the war goes on for ten years, the need for a town hall will not grow less.' Soon, however, the scheme was deferred and was not debated again until after the armistice.

As soon as the great conflict began, Southampton was officially designated

Sir Sidney Kimber was twice mayor of Southampton and was the driving force behind the Cenotaph, the Civic Centre and the Sports Centre.

The Hartley Institute in the early twentieth century, when it was suggested as a possible site for a new town hall. With the university's relocation to Highfield, the building would never find another meaningful use, and it was demolished in the 1930s.

Britain's Military Embarkation Port No. 1. Over the next four years, the port was used by over 8.5m troops, and transported nearly 1m horses and mules and almost 200,000 vehicles. At times, as many as thirty vessels were leaving every night and the average daily cost of the ammunition passing through the town was £100m. The public were not allowed onto the quaysides to watch the departing ships, as boisterous scenes of 'patriotic fervour' during the Crimean War had seen the police called in and the authorities were keen to avoid similar situations.

Even with the frenzied activity in the port, the local economy suffered something of a depression since the majority of normal shipping was suspended; trade was deeply affected and some unemployment was seen. One sector that flourished, predictably, was ship repair. The Day Summers yard in Northam dealt with almost 400 vessels, while the Thornycroft operation, which had moved to Woolston in 1904, was also kept busy. With some of their husbands and sons fighting overseas, Southampton women took on roles such as tram conductress, and as the war went on rationing – particularly of coal – had a great impact. 'The town took on the semblance of a military camp,' recorded local historian A. Temple Patterson, 'with tents and hutments

The Avenue, Southampton. (Library of Congress, LC-DIG-ppmsc-08848)

covering the Common and troops passing and re-passing down the Avenue and through the Bargate.'

Many that returned from the battlefields of Europe came back to Southampton to be treated at the Royal Victoria Military Hospital on Netley Shore, a location that afforded prime views of the continuing war effort: a Southampton Water 'black with ships'. The hospital had been completed in 1863, after seven years' construction in which Queen Victoria had taken particular interest, it being named in her honour. At her suggestion, a connecting railway line had been opened in 1900 to link the building directly to the main line and thus Southampton. With the enormous influx of wounded during the war, the tiny station at Netley village became the third busiest in the entire country. Night and day trainloads of soldiers were transported from vessels arriving in Southampton docks. The vast and imposing hospital spread further into its grounds in the form of huts and tents as an attempt was made to handle the casualties. Following the Battle of the Somme in 1916 alone, 30,000 flooded into Netley. Recuperating soldiers took the air on the hospital's specially built pier, watching the troopships that were taking yet more men across the Channel in their place. Many thousands, of course, never came back at all.

Despite the enormous accommodation available at Netley Hospital, even more was needed and the solution delayed the intended use of a new building while prolonging the life of an old one. With the Hartley buildings proving less and less suitable for life as a home for higher education, new premises had been sought. The newly renamed University College of Southampton was relocated to Highfield and the first phase of construction was completed in the summer of 1914, with the opening ceremony performed by Viscount Haldane, the Lord Chancellor. However, with the outbreak of war the College Council made the decision to delay the move itself: the Hartley was granted a stay of execution and the new buildings were offered to the War Office for use as an ancillary hospital. The relocation was not fully effected until the autumn of 1919.

To facilitate better transport of equipment across the Channel in 1917 a new jetty was built to the west of the Royal Pier, with a temporary railway line linking it to the West (now Central) station. Among the many items shipped abroad through Southampton were nearly 180,000 motor vehicles, this being the first conflict to take advantage of the age of mechanisation. Indeed, many men gained their first experiences of driving during the war, which led directly to the explosion in the popularity of cars in the coming years.

As the end of the war drew nearer, Town Hall enthusiast Sidney Kimber was elected mayor. The mayor-making ceremony took place at the Audit House on Saturday, 9 November 1918, and among the crowds gathered there, Kimber sensed an 'eager expectation for the coming of peace'. His mayoralty was officially proposed by Frederick Dunsford, who speculated that 'Southampton in the near future would be a greater Southampton than it was today,' and hailed the town's 'national importance', so effectively demonstrated during the course of the First World War. Kimber made a short acceptance speech in which he spoke of his long-term ambition to see the city charter bestowed upon Southampton, but for the forthcoming year he urged every council member of whichever political persuasion 'to direct his energies towards the progress of the town and port'.

Less than two days later, early in the morning of Monday, 11 November 1918, Kimber was told to keep his Audit House telephone line clear and to expect a 'priority Government call'. At 9.45 a.m., the new mayor spoke to the commander-in-chief at Portsmouth Naval Dockyard, passing on word from Prime Minister Lloyd George that the Armistice had been signed that morning, and that from 11 a.m. there would be peace in Europe. Kimber was instructed to 'make a public announcement at the earliest opportunity', and so he made his way to the small balcony on the front of the Audit House overlooking Above Bar Street, by now swarming with townspeople anticipating news.

The crowd fell silent to hear Kimber speak, but having heard the news they 'went stark, staring mad with emotion and delirium. Hats, gloves, newspapers, matchboxes were thrown into the air, cheering was spontaneous and men and women's eyes were moist and wet with streaming, happy tears.' Kimber announced a public holiday for municipal staff and suggested that other employers in the town should do likewise. The mayor and the town magistrates convened at the Police Court in the Bargate at 11 a.m., and Southampton held its first memorial service for the dead. Following this, Kimber was returned to the Audit House, where he was called upon to make several further 'encore' appearances for the massed crowds, who were demanding to see their mayor. A special service of thanksgiving took place at St Mary's church the next night, and many more in churches all across the town.

'Immediately after the signing of the Armistice,' Kimber recorded in his memoirs, 'a widespread desire arose for a visible and enduring expression of grateful remembrance to those of Southampton's sons and daughters who had laid down their lives for King and Country' – more than 2,000 in number. He wanted little time in taking action and called a public meeting to discuss the issue. On Monday, 25 November 1918, the Bargate was packed to capacity for the occasion, with some donations towards the cost of the memorial already received. Kimber spoke of the town's 'sacred duty' to commemorate the fallen, and proposed that the nature of the memorial should be decided by a committee, which would bring its plans before another town's meeting to confirm the choice. Shortly afterwards, Alfred Gutteridge – described by Kimber as 'the leading architect in the town' – suggested that the Corporation contact Edwin Lutyens, arguably the leading architect in the country. Lutyens visited Southampton in January 1919, by which time the War Memorial Fund stood at over £2,000.

The same month, however, an episode that played out in the town reflected another aspect of the end of the war. Around 5,000 soldiers, apparently angered by David Lloyd George's demobilisation policy, had mutinied, setting up a makeshift camp in one of the giant warehouses in the docks and refusing to listen to orders. The man called in to defuse this difficult situation was Air Force General Hugh Trenchard, who the following autumn was one of the pallbearers of the coffin of the Unknown Soldier on its way to Westminster Abbey. Taking up residency at the South Western Hotel, Trenchard learned more of the soldiers' case and found himself somewhat sympathetic, but, nevertheless, set about the task he had been given. He entered the warehouse and attempted to speak to the men, but after a promising start was soon subjected to heckling, and was compelled to admit that 'only the threat of force would move them'. At Trenchard's request, 250 men were sent to assist, including in their number some military policemen, all of whom were issued with rifles and ammunition. The armed troops formed two columns outside the warehouse occupied by the mutineers, with instructions to fire if ordered. Trenchard again attempted to engage the men and this time, after the resistance of one sergeant had been dealt with, they acceded to his power. Subsequent investigations revealed that the vast majority of the men had been misled, believing that they were to be discharged upon their arrival in Southampton, when in fact they were intended to be returned to France. Trenchard rounded up the ringleaders, and thus resolved a potentially difficult and dangerous situation.

On a much smaller scale, Mayor Sidney Kimber was soon to find himself contending with similar issues. He was faced with a number of strikes, a manifestation as he saw it of 'internal unrest throughout the country as a result of the termination of the war and lack of co-operation of the employers and workers'. The first incidence of industrial action was undertaken by Corporation workers, who had not received a 5s per week pay increase that they had previously applied for. With no warning, the strike began in July 1919, leaving the town's sewage system unmanned and graves half dug in the cemetery. Faced with such a serious situation, the Corporation acceded to the demands, granted the pay rise, and the strikers were back at work only four days later. The following week the town's bakers went on strike, again with issues about their pay. Although this was a matter involving private companies and their employees, Kimber offered his services as a peacemaker and 'maintained a completely independent attitude to this disagreement'. This time the negotiations were much more difficult and prolonged, with many hours of conferences, but ultimately with the mayor's input, the dispute was successfully resolved.

Better news was forthcoming that year in other areas, particularly with regard to the port trade. The Cunard Line, the great rival of White Star, had first brought its ships to Southampton during the Boer War and had relocated its Canadian service there before the First World War, at around the same time that the Royal Mail Company had greatly expanded its number of routes operating from the port. Now, in 1919, Cunard also transferred its New York services to the south coast: *Aquitania* made the inaugural crossing in June, carrying 5,000 Canadian troops. The move further intensified competition with the White Star Line and helped to ensure that Southampton's post-war malaise was far less serious than that of many of the country's other ports. While cargo ships found themselves in scant demand elsewhere (including, ironically, on Merseyside), passenger trade kept Southampton's commerce at steady and even expanding levels.

Local morale was further boosted by the rise to prominence of the heavyweight boxer, Joe Beckett, whose exploits captured the imagination and the enthusiasm of many townspeople. Born in Wickham, Beckett had begun boxing before the Great War and had achieved mixed results, but 1919 was to be the year that defined his career. In February, he had become Commonwealth champion by defeating the formidable Bombardier Billy Wells, a great boxer who would later find fame sounding the gong depicted at the start of many J. Arthur Rank films. Beckett then dispatched Lonsdale Belt holder, Frank Goddard, in July to become British champion, after which Sidney Kimber and thousands of others gave him a rapturous reception upon his return to Southampton station the following evening.

Beckett's next opponent was the highly regarded American, Eddie McGoorty, and in September Kimber journeyed to London's Olympia stadium to witness the match. A capacity crowd of 20,000 attended, although few of them as luxuriously as Kimber, who sat in the royal box along with the famous Lord Lonsdale. A classic fight ensued, with Beckett the eventual victor by way of a knockout in the seventeenth round. Kimber visited the winning boxer in his dressing room after the contest, 'and conveyed the town's congratulations'. The victory brought with it the opportunity to take on the French champion, Georges Carpentier, with the winner likely to travel to America to fight the seemingly indomitable world champion, Jack Dempsey.

On 4 December 1919, Beckett again took to the ring at Olympia for one of the most anticipated contests in the sport. Back in Southampton, enormous crowds gathered outside the *Daily Echo* offices in Above Bar Street to hear the result of the fight as soon as it was known. The throng was not kept waiting for long: Carpentier knocked out the Englishman after only seventy-four seconds, a sensational outcome for all the wrong reasons. 'The fact of Beckett's amazing defeat was received as one would hear tidings of an unrealisable calamity,' observed the *Daily Echo*, while the *New York Times*, awaiting confirmation of Dempsey's next opponent, reported a victory 'earned by clear superiority'. Beckett continued to box, but his career never again reached the heights that would allow him another chance to fight for the world title. He did, however, retain both his British and Commonwealth crowns until retiring after a second defeat to Carpentier in 1923, again in the first round.

⚜

As the town's economy recovered in the aftermath of the war, the incorporation of more neighbouring districts into the borough was brought up. The suggestion was first made in a speech by the apparently ubiquitous Kimber, in 1918, when he proposed the inclusion of Woolston, Sholing, Bitterne, Swaythling and Bassett, asserting that the policy would enable Southampton to 'advance in stature and prosperity'. The proposal was approved by the Council and, as with the previous extension in 1895, a Local Government Board inquiry set about assessing the case. The hearing was held at the Bargate in January 1920, with witnesses called including the Corporation's medical officer of health, Kimber himself and a representative of the Edwin Jones & Co. retail store, who voiced support for the inclusion of Bassett. After three days, the government inspector closed the proceedings and retired to consider his verdict. In May 1920, a

An aerial view of the River Itchen showing the floating bridge and the dense industry on the shores, *c.*1920.

positive response was received and, in July, the associated bill passed success-fully through Parliament. As a result of the boundary extension the borough almost doubled in acreage and over 31,000 people were added to the existing population of 130,000. At the local elections that November (when Kimber's two year tenure as mayor came to an end), four new alderman and twelve new councillors took their places on the town's administrative body.

The plans to construct a war memorial to commemorate the Sotonians lost during the First World War had progressed over the previous two years, and as the winter of 1920 approached, the cenotaph was nearly complete. Although some had suggested that a town hall could serve this purpose (a course of action pursued in Sheffield among other places), Sidney Kimber rejected the idea and the war memorial committee agreed. It was thought that the memorial should be of an ornamental rather than utilitarian nature, and this decision was con-firmed by a meeting of the townspeople in 1919. Having agreed to design the monument, Sir Edwin Lutyens had originally envisaged the cenotaph in the

Southampton Cenotaph, 2011.

middle of Above Bar Street between Watts Park and East Park, with a small section of both parks cut away on either side to create a surround. However, this scheme was considered too expensive and would have necessitated upheaval to the tramlines. Thus, the location was moved slightly to the west, at the entrance to Watts Park, and, in September 1919, Lutyens's design was almost unanimously approved at a public meeting in the Bargate. A tender of £8,500 was accepted from Messrs Holloway Bros of Westminster and, in early 1920, construction began.

The monument itself took the form of a 55ft-high pylon of Portland stone, recessed on three sides where 2,008 names were inscribed. On the remaining side were a cross and a sword and surmounting the block was the figure of the Unknown Soldier, his face not visible from ground level. Flanking the memorial were two piers capped with fir cones (architectural symbols of eternity) and to the west was the stone of remembrance bearing words selected from the Bible by Rudyard Kipling: 'Their name liveth for evermore.' The design would in effect serve as a prototype for the London cenotaph constructed in Whitehall.

Kimber invited the Lord Lieutenant of Hampshire, Major-General J.E.B. Seely, to perform the unveiling ceremony, which took place on Saturday,

6 November 1920. A procession comprising members of the Council and other local dignitaries made its way from the Central Library to the cenotaph where a large crowd waited, with the relatives of those named on the memorial given honorary places. Kimber then made a speech in which he reflected upon the wishes of the townspeople to commemorate 'the imperishable and heroic devotion unto death of Southampton's fallen sons'. He asked Seely to unveil the monument, achieved by pulling a cord, which removed a canvas covering. After his own speech, Seely pulled a Union Jack from the effigy of the Unknown Soldier, whereupon the last post was sounded and the two minutes' silence impeccably observed. Kimber placed the first wreath at the foot of the cenotaph and many hundreds more followed him. As he so eloquently recorded in his memoirs, 'Rich and poor, wives, mothers, fathers, brothers and sisters of the fallen mingled together and laid their gifts of flowers … Hour after hour they came, the lovely garden spreading and spreading into the parks, until the darkness deepened, and many with proud and humble tears knelt and offered their prayers.'

In the eyes of some people, RMS *Titanic* claimed one of her victims over fifty years after the tragic sinking in 1912. Although he was born in Liverpool in 1887, Fleet lived in Southampton for much of his life. Fleet was been abandoned by his parents at an early age and spent his childhood in orphanages with numerous carers, before he chose a life at sea. He began his navy career in 1903 and worked for several years as the lookout on another White Star vessel, the *Oceanic*. Coincidentally, *Oceanic* was one of the ships that *Titanic* would pass on her departure from Southampton, and was very close to the near collision between the maiden liner and the *New York*. On the fateful night of 14 April 1912, Fleet was at his post in *Titanic*'s crow's nest when he saw the iceberg and immediately rang to alert the bridge, famously declaring, 'Iceberg, right ahead!' As the ship began to sink, Fleet was given the job of crewing one of the lifeboats and was thus lucky enough to survive the tragedy. At the subsequent inquiry, he stated that the provision of binoculars, which had been left behind, would have enabled him to see the danger earlier and would have potentially averted the disaster. Despite his traumatic experience, Fleet continued to work in the Merchant Navy for many more years, even serving for a prolonged period on *Titanic*'s sister ship, *Olympic*. He retired from the sea in 1935 and later in life worked on newspaper stalls selling the *Daily Echo* on the streets of Southampton. However, Fleet was a troubled man. His underprivileged childhood weighed on his mind and, in his own words, he was 'always in debt'. Moreover, he was never able to conquer the guilt that he felt for the sinking of the *Titanic* – a sense of responsibility for so many lives needlessly lost. When his wife died around Christmas 1964, Frederick Fleet finally gave up and he took his own life the following month. For many years, his grave in Hollybrook cemetery remained unmarked, until, in the 1990s, charitable donations were used to provide a proper headstone.

thirteen

THE NEW DOCKS & CIVIC CENTRE

Southampton's port trade, more important than ever in the wake of the First World War, was set to progress further in the 1920s. In 1922, the Trafalgar Dry Dock had to be enlarged for a second time to allow it to house the SS *Berengaria*, although even then there was a clearance of just 10in between the dock walls and the hull of the ship. The same year, the White Star Dock was renamed Ocean Dock, reflecting the fact that many other lines were now using the facility as well, among them White Star's great rival, Cunard. In 1923, the London and South Western Railway Company, owners of the docks, merged with other companies operating rail services in the region to form the Southern Railway Company. Its enhanced financial weight allowed it to consider extending Southampton's port accommodation to provide more berths, which were becoming ever more necessary.

Originally, it was proposed that new docks would be built at Netley Shore, but the docks and marine manager, Gilbert Szlumper, instead preferred the idea of extending the existing docks to the west. Szlumper took his case to the company directors and the general manager, Sir Herbert Walker, and persuaded them to change their minds. Ambitious plans were soon made involving the granting of an Act of Parliament allowing the expenditure of some £13m on reclaiming land from the shallow mudlands lying between Millbrook and the Royal Pier. A retaining wall was to be built extending for 2 miles, while the dredging of Southampton Water was to create a deeper channel and provide the material to fill in the reclaimed area – a larger acreage than that originally enclosed by the ancient town walls. At the western end of the new docks there was to be the world's largest dry dock, with the intention to build a second similar dock alongside it in the future.

With this enormous project still in the planning stages, temporary measures were sought to alleviate the growing inadequacies of the existing docks. The entire coastline on the peninsula between the Itchen and Test rivers was already given over to dockland, and the Trafalgar Dock, less than twenty years old, was struggling to accommodate some of the new larger ships. The solution was one that would become a common and yet intriguing sight in the port for a number of years to come. A 60,000 ton, floating dry dock was employed, capable of handling vessels as large as the *Olympic* and *Majestic* at nearly 1,000ft in length and 170ft wide. Its floor area was some 3½ acres, and its electric pumps could lift a liner out of the water in around four hours. The dock was delivered in May 1924 and was officially opened on 27 June by the Prince of Wales (later Edward VIII and then the Duke of Windsor), who sailed into it aboard the steamer, *Duchess of Fife*. The first ship to be dry-docked in it was the *Arundel Castle*, and the dock was used for over fifteen years before being transferred to Portsmouth.

In 1925, the town's Harbour Board was rehoused in striking new offices at Town Quay, which replaced a building nearly forty years old. It had been intended to update the accommodation before the First World War, but the outbreak of the conflict had delayed the plans. The new building was officially opened in September by Earl Jellicoe, who had commanded the British naval fleet at the Battle of Jutland, in 1916. Also in 1925, P&O vessels returned to Southampton on a regular basis – the company having relocated to London over forty years before. In July, the Khyber began operating services to the Far East, having been refitted for that purpose the previous year. Four years later, P&O also established a new service to India from Southampton, and brought its cruise operations back to the port at about the same time.

On 3 January 1927, work began on the new docks scheme that would transform the port forever, and, in 1928, the seeds of another great building project were sown. Sidney Kimber had attempted to provide Southampton with a town hall and new municipal buildings, but plans were put on hold when the First World War broke out, and, despite raising the issue on a number of occasions since, little had changed. Kimber identified the largest obstacle as public opinion: townspeople failed to see a need for the new buildings and many objected to the expenditure of a significant amount of public money when the provision of more housing was seen as a far more worthy and practical cause. Undeterred, Kimber proceeded with the scheme, which had by now evolved into 'an inter-communicating block of four buildings, a Civic Centre', to be located on the Marlands. Herbert Austen-Hall, who had designed a number of municipal buildings including Lambeth and Holborn town halls, was engaged in the dual role of architectural advisor and the assessor of a competition to be held from

Admiral Jellicoe. (Library
of Congress, LC-DIG-
ggbain-16907)

which the most suitable plan would be selected. In Kimber's view, the people of
Southampton would be more likely to accept the scheme if they could see an
impression of what the completed works would look like.

In September 1928, the winner of the competition was announced as Ernest
Webber, a thirty-two-year-old London architect of growing repute. He had
already won a similar competition to design Manchester Art Gallery (although
it would never actually be constructed) and, more pertinently, earlier in 1928,
his plans for Peterborough Town Hall had also been successful. Webber's
design was a harmonious blend of Classical and more modern styles, and
incorporated municipal offices, law courts, an assembly hall and an art gallery
and art school. His budget of just under £400,000, however, did not allow for a
clock tower, which by Webber's own admission would have provided a pleasing

aesthetic flourish. Nevertheless, Austen-Hall declared himself 'completely sat-isfied that the Corporation have attained the object for which the competition was promoted'.

Kimber's next task was to convince his Labour opponents on the Council, who had been the fiercest critics of the scheme: they had advocated the build-ing of new houses to alleviate circumstances in the poorer parts of the town. The stand-off was resolved by means of a pact. Labour councillors agreed to support and promote the Civic Centre on the understanding that 2,000 new houses would be built in the three coming years. The use of public land for the project, meanwhile, had to be approved at a meeting of the townspeople and then ratified by an Act of Parliament. In January 1929, 2,000 people congre-gated to hear the arguments and make their decision, but the vote (only given by a show of hands) was so close that a poll of the town was held at the end of the month. Once again, the result was very close: out of nearly 17,000 votes cast, the scheme was approved by a majority of less than 1,000. In May, the Parliamentary bill was given royal assent, and finally the last obstacle to the construction of Southampton's new municipal buildings was removed.

That summer work began on the substructure of the first block of the Civic Centre, and a year later, the official foundation-stone laying ceremony took place. The task was performed by the Duke of York, whose presence Kimber had managed to secure through a previous association with Rear Admiral, Basil Brooke. The two men had met after the First World War, and Brooke's later role as equerry to the duke allowed Kimber the opportunity to enquire whether the future King George VI would be willing to accept the town's invitation. Brooke brought his influence to bear and the arrangements were made, although the duchess (later Queen Elizabeth the Queen Mother) was unable to attend: she cancelled all her summer engagements because she was pregnant with Princess Margaret, who was born in August.

On the morning of Tuesday, 1 July 1930, the Duke of York arrived at Southampton station and was driven to the Marlands, where the giant steel framework of the municipal offices already dominated the site. Mayor Young read an address of welcome, to which the duke responded – hoping that the completed Civic Centre would 'worthily symbolise all that is best in the Civic, Judicial and Artistic life of the British nation'. Kimber asked the duke to lay the stone, which he duly did, after which the great crowds sang 'O God Our Help In Ages Past', the Isaac Watts hymn that in years to follow would become inextricably linked with the Civic Centre. After completing his

The Duchess of York, the Queen Mother. (Library of Congress, LC-DIG-ggbain-21924)

ceremonial duties, the Duke of York made a number of other appearances in Southampton. First, he travelled to the Royal Pier, both to open the Royal Southampton Horticultural Society show and to view the ongoing works for the £13m scheme to extend the docks. After lunch at the South Western Hotel, the duke laid a wreath at the Southampton Cenotaph and then visited the Ordnance Survey offices in London Road before travelling to Highfield, to open a new hall of residence at the university. After a hectic few hours in Southampton, the duke returned to London by train that afternoon.

As the winter of 1932 approached, the new Municipal Offices block of the Civic Centre was nearing completion, and, on 8 November, the Duke of York returned to Southampton to perform the opening ceremony, this time accompanied by the duchess. Again the royal visitors travelled to the town by train and were transferred by car to the Marlands, where a crowd estimated at 50,000 people – over a quarter of Southampton's population – were eagerly waiting.

Mayor Woolley welcomed the duke and duchess in a ceremony in the new council chamber, and in the duke's speech, he predicted that the Civic Centre would 'not fail to make its due impression upon this and future generations'. He then formally declared the building open before being taken on a tour with Woolley, Sidney Kimber and architect, Ernest Webber, at the end of which he and the duchess made a crowd-pleasing appearance on the small balcony over the main entrance. Additional visits were made, to the cenotaph, before lunch at the South Western Hotel and another inspection of the works at the new docks.

⁓◦ ◦⁓

The following year, the port's enormous new graving dock was completed and on the morning of Wednesday, 26 July 1933, King George V and Queen Mary set sail from Cowes on the royal yacht in order to perform the official opening ceremony. The waterside was thronged with thousands of enthusiastic well-wishers, and many of the other vessels in Southampton Water were decorated with flags and bunting for the occasion. The yacht approached the new dock, which was lined on both sides by four huge grandstands accommodating 11,000 spectators. As the prow of the yacht entered the dock it cut a silken ribbon of red, white and blue, and the Royal Marines Band (on the deck of the yacht) struck up a rendition of Rule, Britannia. 'Cheers volleyed and thundered' as the yacht berthed, and at exactly midday the king, queen and Duke and Duchess of York were piped ashore, to be greeted by J.E.B. Seely, the Lord Lieutenant of Hampshire, who thirteen years earlier had unveiled Southampton's cenotaph. After a number of introductions, the royal visitors walked to the ceremonial dais, where Gerald Loder, chairman of the Southern Railway Company, gave the address of welcome.

Loder reflected that forty-three years before to the day, Queen Victoria had visited Southampton to open the Empress Dock, and that since then the town and port had made enormous progress. He spoke of Southampton's critical role in the First World War and since then its expanding significance as a 'Gateway to the Empire' and indeed the rest of the world – 'a most important link in the chain that binds the Motherland to the Dominions beyond the seas'. The latest extensions, crowned by the largest graving dock ever built, able to house a 100,000-ton vessel, would 'provide for the needs of the world's shipping'. In response, the king spoke warmly of the royal family's long association with Southampton and of his pleasure that he had been invited to perform the day's ceremony. 'From the early days of our overseas trade Southampton has held a foremost place in the commercial life of this country,' he remarked. 'This position it has retained as the result of wise and continuous development, and its record as a port of embarkation during the years of the Great War will never be forgotten.' The king also spoke of his admiration that work had been brought to such successful fruition despite the country's despondent economic state: 'I rejoice to think that the building of this dock has given the blessing of employment to many who would otherwise have been without it.'

After the king had officially named the King George V Graving Dock, the queen christened it by pouring Empire wine from a silver cup into the waters. Dr Cyril Garbett, the Lord Bishop of Winchester, then performed a short service of dedication, which concluded with a rendition of the national anthem. The crowd's cheering resumed as the royal party returned to the yacht and departed for Cowes, to complete the rest of their holiday.

Following the ceremony, the guests retired to Ocean Dock for lunch on board the Cunard liner, *Berengaria*. The chairman of the Cunard Line, Sir Percy Bates, spoke of the company's new super liner, which was half finished on the slipway at the John Brown shipyard on the Clyde. The liner, which at the time was known only as *No. 534*, would make use of the new graving dock along with her proposed sister ship, operating a weekly service between Southampton and New York. Bates acknowledged that construction of the great ship was behind schedule, but refuted allegations of design problems: 'The ship is right, the dock is right, and the worst that can happen is that there will be a little more delay,' he declared.

Ultimately, the new liner's future was assured in circumstances that would alter the history of passenger shipping. The construction of the vessel captured the imagination of the public, and the prospect of her completion provided a fillip in dark economic times. Ramsay MacDonald's coalition government appreciated this, and eventually agreed to finance the rest of the work needed on the ship. There was, however, one important condition to be fulfilled: the merger of the two rival shipping lines Cunard and White Star. After some opposition, the directors of both companies decided to accede to the request in December 1933, at which the government bestowed nearly £10m upon the new combined firm. Of this, £3m would fund the completion of *No. 534* and £5m would pay for a new sister ship, with the remainder to be used as working capital. Royal assent to the union was given in March 1934, and Cunard White Star Limited was officially formed in May. From then on work proceeded

The King George V Graving Dock, also built as part of the docks extension scheme, was at the time the largest dry dock in the world.

swiftly: *No. 534* was launched as the *Queen Mary* in September and completed eighteen months later.

The month before the landmark merger between the Cunard and White Star lines, the second block of Southampton's Civic Centre had been completed and opened. The original plans had, for budgetary reasons, not included a clock tower, much to the disappointment of architect, Ernest Webber, Sidney Kimber and a significant number of the townspeople. However, during the planning stages, an enquiry was made about incorporating the County Courts into the building, and Webber's design revisions, at the behest of the town councillors, made provision for a clock tower and bells. The position of the tower was finalised by flying a miniature barrage balloon at the appropriate height, to give an idea of the scale and aesthetic impact of the construction. Once the balloon was in place, Webber and Kimber drove to various points around the town to gauge how easily it could be seen and from how far away.

On the morning of 7 November 1933, great crowds gathered on Havelock Road in front of the new building, awaiting the opening ceremony. The man charged with the task was the Lord Chancellor, Viscount Sankey, who, accompanied by a procession of Corporation members, arrived at the Law Courts just before 12 p.m. On the hour, the bells sounded the Westminster chimes, followed by a verse of 'O God Our Help In Ages Past', which would thereafter be played four times a day. Sankey then opened the doors using the same key that the Duke of York had used to open the municipal offices, and the procession entered to join the other guests already assembled. The traditional speeches ensued, in which the Lord Chancellor enthused about the town's recent development as being 'directed with a skill and energy which has made Southampton an example of the progress of England'. He also congratulated Webber on his design and paid tribute to 'those who have been responsible for the genesis of this scheme, and for bringing it to a successful issue'.

As the year drew to a close, the town reflected on another period of advancement and development. The worldwide economic downturn may still have been reverberating following the infamous stock market crash of 1929, but Southampton's progress appeared to continue unheeded despite the high levels of local unemployment that had led to a demonstration by 1,400 out of work men, in October 1932. As the novelist and playwright, J.B. Priestley noted in his *English Journey* of late 1933: 'Here was a town that had not let the universal depression master it and that was contriving to enjoy its unique situation, between forest and heath and deep blue water, a lovely bay window upon the wide world.'

Good news for Southampton's workers came the following year with the completion and opening of the Solent Flour Mills, built by Joseph Rank Ltd. The mill stood on part of the land newly reclaimed in the docks extension scheme, and was powered by electricity and featured the latest technological advancements in the industry. The building began its operational life in August 1934 and was formally opened in a ceremony conducted by the mayor in October. It has been altered and extended over the years, and remains an imposing sight on Southampton's waterside vista to this day.

In the town centre, meanwhile, more new building work was under way relating to the Civic Centre scheme. The plans necessitated the demolition of Thorner's Almshouses, a charity founded in 1787 to care for widows and needy children, and its relocation to the Regent's Park area of the town. The vacated Above Bar site was used to create a new wider road towards the railway station and new docks, with the remaining land sold for the construction of a cinema and shops. The Forum cinema was opened by Mayor Waller in June 1935, and provided nearly 2,000 seats. With film going still extremely popular, following

Games aboard the *Mauretania* in 1911. (Library of Congress, LC-USZ62-118048)

the golden age of Hollywood in the 1920s, cinemas were springing up all over Southampton. Only a few hundred yards away was the Regal (later the Odeon), opened a year earlier, while in Commercial Road there was the seven-year-old Empire, later renamed the Gaumont and then the Mayflower. The suburbs too had their own 'picture palaces', such as the Art Deco Plaza that opened in Northam Road in 1932 and Portswood's Broadway, opened two years earlier.

While growing emphasis was given to the leisure pursuits of townspeople, Southampton's industrial prosperity was still reliant primarily on port trade. However, as attention turned to the new era in shipping that the *Queen Mary* would bring, time had run its course for some of the town's greatest liners. On 1 July 1935, the popular *Mauretania*, the first ship to use the new docks, left for the last time, bound for the scrapyard at Rosyth. A shadow of her former self, unused for months and with her masts cut down to allow passage under the Forth Bridge, her departure reduced some of the watching crowds to tears. Meanwhile, the *Olympic* had been berthed in the new docks since April, and at 4.30 p.m. on 11 October 1935, she slipped away from the quayside for the last time, bound for a breaker's yard in Jarrow. Almost identical in appearance to her ill-fated sister, *Titanic*, the *Olympic* had, after an unconvincing start, enjoyed an illustrious career, earning the nickname 'Old Reliable'. Until the launch of *Queen Mary*, she had remained the largest British-built liner afloat, and had become a friendly and familiar sight in Southampton's docks. Notably, the coverage of *Olympic*'s departure in the *Daily Echo* contained no mention of *Titanic*.

On 27 March 1936, *Queen Mary* entered Southampton Water for the first time, greeted by tens of thousands of eager spectators. She had been anchored off Cowes since early that morning, leaving at 12.37 p.m. to make for the King George V Graving Dock, which had been specially constructed to house her. Southampton was festooned in bunting and flags for the event, and people travelled from all over the country to witness the arrival of a ship that was a legend even before her maiden voyage. Hundreds of other vessels populated the waters, from liners to dinghies, many of them used as vantage points for spectators. Thousands more 'gasped in wonderment from the shore' while aeroplanes swooped and rolled in the skies above in salute. Under the banner headline 'Wonder Ship Comes Home', the *Daily Echo* rightly described the occasion as 'an epoch making event in Southampton's long and honoured history as a port'. The *Queen Mary* had arrived, and so had the golden age of passenger shipping.

Advances in ocean-going transport were not the only ones being made at the time, although developments in air travel were in a rather different field. A few weeks before the arrival of the *Queen Mary* a small fighter plane had been given its first test flight at Eastleigh Aerodrome just north of Southampton. The man at the controls was Captain Joseph Summers, the chief test pilot for Vickers, who had also flown prototypes designed by Barnes Wallis, and the aircraft was the Spitfire – destined for greatness that its creator, R.J. Mitchell, would not live to see. Initial flights led to some adjustments, but the design was so successful that only three months after the first trial, the Air Ministry placed an order for over 300 Spitfires at a cost of nearly £1.5m. Production began at Vickers Supermarine factory in Woolston – a sensational boost for the local economy – but in time proved to be too much for a company already manufacturing Mitchell's designs of a flying boat. Owing to a number of problems, the first production Spitfire was not completed at Vickers until nearly two years after the placing of the order, and plans were put in place to augment manufacture at a secondary location in the Midlands. The value to the nation of this small aircraft would in the coming years be greater than anyone could possibly have imagined.

Work on the Civic Centre, meanwhile, had slowed because of financial problems: the first two blocks had cost significantly more than expected and

Cunard liner *Queen Mary* arrives in the King George V Dock for the first time, March 1936.

South Shore, Southampton. (Library of Congress, LC-DIG-ppmsc-08847)

governmental approval had to be obtained to continue with the project. Nearly three and a half years after the opening of the Law Courts, the third section, the Assembly Hall, was finally completed. In recognition of the history of the room in the Bargate previously used for public meetings, it was to be known as the Guildhall. The opening ceremony took place on 13 February 1937 and was undertaken by seventy-one-year-old Lord Derby, the president of the Association of Municipal Corporations, who was descended from the family that gave its name to the famous horse race. A ceremonial procession formed at the municipal offices and made its way to the Guildhall, where Geoffrey Webber, the son of architect Ernest Webber, presented Lord Derby with a gold key that he used to unlock the great doors. After the unveiling of a commemorative stone, the party entered the main hall – already filled with guests – for the speeches. Mayor Chick talked of the new buildings 'befitting the town and port which, I sincerely believe, is destined to become the greatest in the country', while Lord Derby described the hall as 'not only modern in its conception, but beautiful as any I have lately seen constructed'. Sidney Kimber, who had been knighted in 1935, also spoke, and at various points in the proceedings, the Guildhall's magnificent new organ was played by the eminent organist Dr George Thalben-Ball, who had also advised on its design.

The Civic Centre was not the only municipal project in which Kimber immersed himself in the 1930s. His second grand scheme was the town's sports centre, which he had first advocated to the Council in September 1930, envisaging a facility of nearly 300 acres situated between Bassett and Lordswood. Initially, however, councillors rejected the idea, and it was nearly three years before approval was gained, requiring (as with the Civic Centre) the compliance of the Labour members. The golf courses were opened in September 1935, and two and a half years later the entire scheme neared completion. Before the opening there were what now seem to be quaintly antiquated discussions about 'the advisability, or otherwise, of all games being played on Sundays'. The decision was taken that sport on a Sunday was indeed permissible, but only after 2 p.m.

The official opening of the sports centre took place in May 1938 and was performed by the Duke and Duchess of Kent. 'You have provided facilities for a very great number of sports,' declared the duke, 'and I feel sure that these facilities will prove a great attraction to the fortunate inhabitants of the borough of Southampton.' The completed centre, although slightly smaller than in Kimber's original vision because of the sale of some land, nevertheless incorporated excellent provision for sport in the town. It included cricket, football and hockey pitches, tennis courts, bowling greens and a running track, as well as the golf courses, changing rooms and a pavilion. As Kimber noted, it was 'a perpetual source of health giving enjoyment for all those who wish to avail themselves of it and a priceless possession for the years to come'.

Kimber was also closely involved in the new buildings of the King Edward VI School, constructed at the same time as the sports centre. The school was originally founded in 1553 with a bequest in the will of William Capon, a Cambridge-educated man who served as the rector of St Mary's church. Its first location was in Winkle Street, and, in 1696, it moved to the ancient West Hall. After over a century it moved again, this time to Bugle Street, which was where Kimber himself attended the school until he was fourteen. With student numbers increasing yet another site was sought and new buildings on the western edge of the Marlands opened in 1896. They again proved insufficient to meet the requirements of the day, and after the First World War, the school governors purchased 11 acres of land on Hill Lane adjacent to the Common. Ernest Berry Webber, architect of the Civic Centre, was engaged to design the new school, and it was formally opened in November 1938.

Less than six months later the Civic Centre was also completed, over ten years since Webber's design had been selected. Like the Guildhall, the Art Block had been delayed owing to financial reasons, although some of the funding was provided by the generous bequest of Robert Chipperfield, the former chairman of the Grammar School governors, who had laid the foundation stone of the school built overlooking the Marlands. Upon his death in 1911, Chipperfield left a significant legacy to the town, to be put towards the furtherance of art. As with many aspects of the Civic Centre's construction, lengthy debate raged over the use of the funds, generally centring over whether the money should be spent purely on works of art or if part of it could finance the building itself. Ultimately, the cash was divided, and a second bequest from Frederick Smith added more works to the collection. Again, changes had been made to the original plans, this time allowing the inclusion of a new library to replace the forty-five-year-old building almost directly opposite on the other side of West Park.

The opening ceremony of the art block took place on 26 April 1939, conducted by the Duke and Duchess of Gloucester. Appropriately, and as for all the ceremonial occasions connected with the construction of the Civic Centre, the townspeople turned out in force. They lined the route taken by the royal visitors' car from the station to the Marlands, and at times spirits ran so high that the crowds had to be restrained. Upon reaching the gallery, the party gathered at the entrance steps, where Webber handed the duke the key that had been used to open the first three blocks. Inside, the formalities continued, and the duchess unveiled a portrait of Kimber – an anonymously donated gift, painted by the artist T.C. Dugdale. After the duchess had also unveiled a commemorative stone in the entrance hall, the entire party transferred to the Guildhall, again creating a commotion in the onlooking crowds.

Several speeches were made, including Mayor Powdrill's brief history of the entire project, in which he observed that the years of delays had ultimately been beneficial. If the buildings had been constructed when the suggestion was first made they would probably have proved inadequate already, and the whole issue would have arisen once more. The duke spoke of his pride at helping to complete the project inaugurated by his brother the king almost nine years earlier, describing 'a centre of usefulness and dignity which will enable you to welcome in fitting manner all who come within your gates'. Nearly thirty years after he had first suggested it, Kimber's grand scheme was finally finished.

The completed Civic Centre provided accommodation for all of the town's administrative departments, Council Chamber, conference rooms and mayor's suite. There were three courts, a police station and cells, and of course the clock tower, which is still a prominent and recognisable part of Southampton's skyline. The Guildhall offered an assembly hall that the town could be proud of, which had already proved popular when staging musical concerts and even, on occasion, plays. Finally, the art block included the gallery, art school and library. Architectural historian Nikolaus Pevsner enthusiastically described the scheme as 'perhaps the most ambitious civic building erected in the provinces during the inter-war years, a symbol of Southampton's heyday as a port, prospering while much of the rest of the country was in the darkness of a slump'. While the town's spirits were high in light of the royal visit, however, a dark cloud hung over the country. As well as its coverage of the art gallery opening ceremony, that afternoon's *Daily Echo* also reported that Britain was 'ready for talks with Germany', and that on that very day Prime Minister Neville Chamberlain had proposed conscription for all men between twenty and twenty-one years of age. That spring day the Civic Centre had attracted crowds from far and wide; within eighteen months it would become a target for bombs.

ERNEST BERRY WEBBER, ARCHITECT

The architect of Southampton Civic Centre, Ernest Berry Webber, was born in 1896 in the Walworth district of London, not far from the Oval cricket ground. He learnt his trade by training with and assisting a number of prominent architects of the day, the best known of whom was probably Emanuel Vincent Harris, a man devoted to the Classical style of design who constructed several substantial public buildings. Webber's apprenticeship was interrupted by his service as a guardsman in the First World War, but upon his return to civilian life, he soon began to enter architectural competitions in his own right. In August 1920, his design for Sheffield Memorial Hall was placed third – the winning architect, ironically, was Vincent Harris. Work on the building would not begin until 1928, the year of Webber's success with Southampton Civic Centre, but its influence on the Guildhall block is plain. In the meantime, Webber became an Associate of the Royal Institute of British Architects in 1923 and three years later set up his own private practice. His participation in architectural competitions increased and many of his designs were highly placed: his winning design for Peterborough Town Hall was described as the work of a man 'at the top of his form' in *Architect & Building News*. Most of Webber's prominent completed works were also municipal buildings, including Hammersmith Town Hall, Dagenham Civic Centre and the post-war reconstruction of Portsmouth Town Hall. However, several of his projects were abandoned or delayed because of the economic restraints of the 1930s, and the advent of the Second World War naturally curtailed new building schemes. With the arrival of peace in Europe, Webber achieved some further success, seeing his designs for the Royal Naval Barracks in Devonport and Nuffield United Services Officers' Club in Portsmouth come to fruition. However, many other projects (such as municipal buildings in Reading and even Zimbabwe, and an entire town centre plan for Darlington in County Durham) never came to pass. With better luck and timing, many more of Ernest Webber's buildings might have graced the towns and cities of Britain, and he might have achieved a far greater level of recognition. Webber retired to Brighton in the 1950s and died there, little remembered, in 1963.

fourteen

BLOODIED BUT UNBEATEN

In the summer of 1939, as the Second World War drew inexorably closer, Southampton was an active and prosperous town, with 20m tons of shipping passing through its docks every year. In the event of war, it once again expected to be made the country's primary embarkation port, and with this in mind, preparations began long before Germany's fateful invasion of Poland. Five years earlier, Southampton's waterworks engineer had spoken to the Ministry of Health (at the time also heavily involved in the ongoing financing and construction of the Civic Centre) and the Air Council. Under discussion was a contingency plan to protect the town's water supply in the advent of an air attack, and measures were in place by the autumn of 1938. That summer the first blackout exercise in the country had taken place in Southampton, and the following July the townspeople were provided with nearly 10,000 air-raid shelters and 100 basement shelters. Precautions were also taken to ensure that supplies of food would be as unaffected as possible, in line with a scheme created by the government Food Department. The plan organised food retailers into groups, all of whom agreed that if any were incapacitated by enemy action the others would attempt to fill the void until the damaged business could be reinvigorated. Additionally, contingencies were put in place providing stores of emergency food, both in the town itself and in nearby rural areas.

When the war officially broke out on 3 September, 14,000 children were evacuated almost immediately, mainly to homes in north Hampshire, Dorset and Somerset. With curious logic, some children from Portsmouth were actually evacuated into Southampton. One outbound Southampton evacuee recalled, 'We thought it was a big adventure going on a train and never realised it was going to be four years for those people that stayed down there.' The rationing of petrol had an immediate impact, the result being that as soon as October 1939 horses and carts were once more becoming common sights in the streets.

As was the case with many other ports and coastal towns in the South of England, Southampton had its part to play in the Dunkirk operation of May 1940. Many vessels from the port, famously differing vastly in size, took part in the evacuation of forces from northern France. Two cross-Channel steamers owned by the Southern Railway Company, *Lorina* and *Normannia*, were unfortunate enough not to return from the mission. Red Funnel steamers were also called up to assist with the war effort, although the *Gracie Fields*, described by J.B. Priestley as 'the pride of our ferry service to the Isle of Wight', was struck by dive-bombers and sank at Dunkirk. But Churchill's resilience, as evident from his statement, 'If this long island story of ours is to end at last, let it end only when each one of us lies choking in his own blood upon the ground', was reflected in the outcome of the operation. The government had hoped that 50,000 soldiers might be rescued, so the actual total of over 300,000, two thirds of whom were British, was nothing short of miraculous. In the aftermath of such optimism, however, greater upheaval and distress were to come the following month, when the beginning of the Blitz brought the war into the streets of Southampton and the homes of its people.

The first air raid came on 19 June 1940, but this one and its immediate successors over the next few weeks were comparatively small. That month Southampton received many evacuees from the soon to be occupied Channel Islands and, in turn, more of the town's own children were evacuated ahead of the forthcoming raids. On 13 August, the first heavy and concentrated attacks on the docks took place. The International Cold Storage warehouse was hit – a giant target 400ft long and 100ft wide that had been built in 1900. With more than 2,000 tons of butter inside, it burned for several days before the flames could be extinguished. Over the next two weeks the old docks and some of the town's suburbs were targeted, including St Mary's, Woolston and Portswood. In the centre of Southampton, meanwhile, the town's oldest buildings were converted for use as shelters. The Bargate was adapted, its great arch bricked up, as was the Undercroft at the top of Bugle Street. Even those regions with a low residential population had to have appropriate shelter accommodation to deal with the numbers that could be present in the area in the course of a normal day. 'The public shelter was for everybody,' recalled one witness, 'it was always open and you just dived in there.'

September brought escalating rumours of German preparations for invasion and with them the heaviest and most intensive bombing raids yet. In the first two weeks of the month there were seven attacks and shortly afterwards

The docks were a primary target. The International Cold Storage warehouse continued to burn for several days after being hit.

German planes began to concentrate their efforts on the shipyards and related industries on the Itchen shores. The Woolston area was bombarded and eventually, on 26 September, the bombers achieved the primary aim of their onslaught in that area: the Vickers Supermarine works on the banks of the river was all but destroyed. The repercussions could have been even worse if Spitfires had still been entirely manufactured in the plant, as they had been the previous year. As it was, supplementary production was already under way at Castle Bromwich in Birmingham, with extra work undertaken in and around Southampton, and manufacture was not too badly affected. Other local engineering firms also gave themselves over to the war effort, repairing army vehicles, for example.

A brief hiatus in the attacks followed, but when they resumed yet another threat was unleashed. In October 1940, the Pirelli General Cable Works in Western Esplanade was bombed. This was another strategic manufacturing site. Many women were employed in the plant, and when the bombs fell and the workers made for cover, they faced a hail of bullets. One witness recalled, 'You often heard about the Germans machine gunning people and they actually did, and I actually seen it done that afternoon. They actually did machine gun them women as they run out from the side doors towards the shelters.'

Of course, the bombs did not discriminate. On 6 November, fourteen children were killed while taking a class at the School of Art in the Art Block of the Civic Centre, itself only completed and opened eighteen months before. In fact, the building had apparently been specifically earmarked for attack by Herman Göring, commander-in-chief of the Luftwaffe, who likened it to a cake. That November day one of Göring's most decorated flying aces, Helmut Wick, was in the air over Southampton, although it is not known if

Other warehouses were reduced to shells. (Courtesy of Associated British Ports)

he was directly involved in the attack on the Civic Centre. Below him, children from the Central District Girls' School, aged between eleven and thirteen, were taking a needle and thread lesson when the sirens sounded. They were rushed to a makeshift basement shelter, but one of the twelve bombs smashed through the two floors above and directly into their hiding place. Of the girls from Central, only one survived, her injuries necessitating months of recovery in hospital. Another twenty-one people in and near the Civic Centre died in the attack, including Grace Lanham, the wife of the building's superintendent. Also injured was their daughter Audrey, who was buried up to her waist in debris, unable to see or hear her mother: 'In spite of my repeated calls to her, there was no response. It was some time later that her body was found.'

Two and a half weeks later, on 23 November, the town was targeted again in a brutal raid by over 100 bombers; this began at 6.15 p.m. and did not end until 7.30 a.m. The Germans dropped at least 800 bombs and 4,000 incendiaries, although these figures are considered by some to be an underestimation. By dawn, nearly 80 people had died and 300 were injured. The Civic Centre was struck again, and 'much of the town's main business and shopping centre was set on fire and thousands were rendered homeless'. The *Daily Echo* observed that 'the raiders lit the sky with flares, then dropped showers of incendiaries and high explosive bombs on widely separated parts of the town'. One family, having seen their previous home destroyed the week before, was bombed again, and they were trapped in the rubble for three hours before being rescued by a policeman. Displaying the resilience that would become famous over the course of the conflict, the family 'started singing to keep up our spirits'.

Despite all this, as far as was possible people endeavoured to carry on as normal. The Edwin Jones department store advertised its hair salon as able to be evacuated in only three minutes in the event of an air raid. With a minimum of disruption, customers would be transferred to a basement salon, where coiffuring continued 'throughout the warning period'. However, hard as it might have been for the people of Southampton to believe, worse was still to come. On the consecutive nights of Saturday, 30 November and Sunday, 1 December, the town was pounded with bombs and incendiaries as never before, in raids lasting up to seven hours. Early on the Saturday evening, a single bomb landed in the High Street. It heralded a tirade of explosives, with enemy planes first dropping parachute flares to illuminate their targets and facilitate more accurate bombing. Bernard Knowles recorded: 'Even the most savage convulsion of nature could convey no idea of the universal uproar and clamour.

The Edwin Jones department store was barely identifiable as a building: all that remained was a mass of twisted wreckage.

Every possible form of terror was present.' The bombs were fewer in number than on the previous Saturday, but greater in weight. Nearly 6,000 properties were damaged or destroyed, among them the Ordnance Survey offices, the Rank Flour Mill and the Edwin Jones department store. When the planes returned the following night to continue the carnage, some of the fires were still burning. That weekend 137 people died in Southampton, many of them in shelters that the bombs simply tore through.

As Monday morning dawned, the extent of the damage to the town became all too clear. Its central spine of the High Street and Above Bar Street 'had largely crumbled into unrecognisable wreckage'. Standing almost alone among the piles of rubble and twisted steel was the Bargate – an iconic symbol of defiance, perhaps, in the same way that St Paul's Cathedral would be in London. Fires that could not be tackled because of damage to the water supply consumed many more buildings – the worst of the blazes could be seen from Cherbourg – and huge numbers of homes and businesses were without gas and electricity.

In Above Bar Street the *Daily Echo* offices and the Palace Theatre were badly damaged.

Many who were unwilling or simply unable to face another night's bombard-
ment fled to the surrounding areas, securing their homes as well as they could
and hoping for the best. Those with nowhere to go went anyway: 'On foot, with
prams and pushcarts containing their scanty bedding, men, women and children trudged into the night to sleep in schools, barns or outhouses, or wander
in the woods till morning.'

The Southampton they returned to was increasingly devastated and the
spiritual refuges of many, the town's churches, were especially badly affected.
St Mary's, Holy Rood and the Unitarian church on London Road were nothing but ruins, while the neo-Classical splendour of All Saints' was so severely
damaged that it was not rebuilt. In the aftermath of the blitzkrieg, some of the
townspeople were so irreparably scarred by their experiences and what they had
witnessed that they took their own lives. Although these cases may have been
the exception rather than the rule, the morale of the people of Southampton
was unquestionably (and understandably) battered by the Blitz. Cyril Garbett,
the Bishop of Winchester, came to the town early in December and observed, 'I
went from parish to parish and everywhere there was fear.'

On 5 December the town's spirits were lifted to a certain extent by the arrival of King George VI in a visit 'shorn of pomp and pageantry by the grimness of war,' but 'yet noble; the intimate meeting of a king with his people'. The monarch, accompanied by the minister of home security, Herbert Morrison, arrived at the Civic Centre, the building that he had inaugurated as the Duke of York in 1930. Gathered there and overlooked by 'shattered windows and pitted stonework', were various members of the Civil Defence Services, with one lady especially presented to the king for a recent act of heroism. Mrs Frances Hartley, an ambulance driver since the start of the war, had risked her own life to go to the assistance of two wounded soldiers during a German attack, with 'bombs raining down all around'. The king was then introduced to a number of civic dignitaries, including Sidney Kimber and Percy Lanham, the superintendent of the Civic Centre, whose wife had been killed a month earlier. After a tour of the Civic Centre, the king made several other stops around Southampton, and walked down Above Bar Street while men still worked to clear away the rubble at the side of the road. He departed, having offered

In December 1940, King George VI visited the town.

'sympathy with the town in its sufferings and congratulated the townspeople on their spirit'.

At the start of the following week the *Daily Echo* described a Southampton that bore 'the mark of the beast', consisting of 'mountains of rubble' and 'piles of ashes'. But with stirring rhetoric the newspaper attempted to galvanise its readers:

> Everybody who fought to save life and property deserves the highest honour that can be given ... They helped by giving homes to the homeless; by organising emergency feeding centres; by carrying on as usefully as they could. They were grim, many were angry, many were in tears, but they were not beaten ... Such a town can never be destroyed.

A Mass Observation report at around the same time recorded the scene, and noted that 'public utilities are still seriously affected. Thousands of homes have broken windows and leaking roofs which make them extremely unpleasant, if not uninhabitable.'

In the course of December, further attacks focused on the docks and two large quayside warehouses were obliterated. Two Isle of Wight steamers were sunk while in dock, although one of them, *Duchess of Cornwall*, was salvaged, repaired and brought back into service. Towards the end of the month, a tug was sunk after being struck by bombs, while two destroyers being built at the Thornycroft yard were also hit and badly damaged. In general, however, the year ended comparatively quietly, with none of the raids approaching the destruction levels seen at the start of December. By New Year's Eve, there were signs that Southampton was beginning to find its feet again; hope was starting to spread that the darkest days had been endured. As the final moments of 1940 ticked by, this feeling was reflected by events at Holy Rood church, where townspeople had traditionally gathered to recognise the passing of another year. With the church a ruined shell and the bells blasted from their housings, there seemed little hope that the citizens of Southampton would make their annual pilgrimage, but, albeit in depleted numbers, come they did. There they stood together and sang 'Auld Lang Syne', 'There'll Always Be An England' and the town's hymn 'O God Our Help In Ages Past'. One witness of this touching scene recalled that 'the spirit of the people was wonderful. As the old year waned I seemed to see a light shining over Holy Rood ... Although Hitler may have wrecked our buildings, he has not wrecked us.'

The same sentiments were abundant a month later, on 31 January 1941, when Southampton welcomed another morale-boosting visitor, this time Prime Minister Winston Churchill. For security reasons his arrival had not been widely announced, so when his car drew up at the Civic Centre that morning many bystanders were taken aback. Predictably, however, word of the prime minister's appearance soon spread, and, before long, he, Mrs Churchill and President Roosevelt's envoy, Harry Hopkins, had attracted a sizeable crowd. To cheers from the assembled onlookers, Churchill began an inspection of civil defence forces on the Civic Centre forecourt. Throughout the visit, Britain's great war leader was in good spirits and smiling congenially – no doubt reassuring the townspeople. For only one brief moment did his smile leave him. The inspection over, Churchill climbed the steps of the municipal offices and turned to the throng with a solemn countenance. 'Are we downhearted?' he boomed.

Winston Churchill visited soon after, in January 1941. (Courtesy of Associated British Ports)

'A moment afterwards,' related the *Daily Echo*, 'came the answering cry of the crowd; "NO!" – and Mr Churchill smiled again.'

The optimism was to some extent justified: the intensity of the bombings during the winter of 1940 was, mercifully, not to be repeated. Throughout 1941, there were twenty-six attacks on Southampton in which over 100 people were killed and nearly 400 injured. On 11 March, Above Bar Street was bombed again, resulting in the loss of twenty-two lives, and two nights later a further raid struck the British American Tobacco factory in Millbrook, which was soon ablaze. Meanwhile, in Portswood, an enormous bomb landed on a car garage, throwing many of the vehicles there into the air and leaving a crater 33ft in diameter. Cars landed in the surrounding gardens, with one of them coming to rest upside down on top of an air-raid shelter. Despite being only 23ft from where the explosive landed and having had their shelter destroyed by a flying car, all the occupants survived. That month the German media claimed that Southampton was the fourth most heavily bombed English town, with only London, Liverpool and Birmingham more badly affected.

In April, a German Heinkel bomber was shot down in an air battle over the town and crashed in the Inner Avenue area. Miraculously no residents were killed, but two of the four German airmen, who abandoned their aircraft in its descent, did not survive. The following month a brief but deadly raid took place in the early hours of one morning. Only twelve bombs fell but they claimed ten lives, with a number of victims in Albert Road buried alive; a ten-hour rescue operation ensued. The savagery of the 1941 raids did not equal those of the previous year, but two of them came close. Early one June morning, the town was attacked with parachute mines, resulting in nineteen deaths and many more injuries. The following month 150 bombs and 5,000 incendiaries were dropped, causing 38 deaths and over 100 injuries. In September, a German radio report announced that Southampton had been almost entirely destroyed and left as 'a smoking ruin'. The town's residents, of course, knew that the claim was exaggerated and the propaganda probably only served to strengthen their resolve. Furthermore, owing to Hitler's vain pursuit of the conquest of Russia, it would be six months before Southampton was attacked again.

In 1942, a new telephone exchange was built in the docks, the previous building having been destroyed earlier in the conflict. Known as N Vault, the replace-ment exchange was a huge concrete block, partially submerged, with walls thick enough to withstand heavy bombings. Also in 1942, Southampton's port trade finally began to recover from the torpor brought about by the war. Over a million

The suburbs were also seriously affected, as these houses in Manor Road illustrate.

tons of commercial freight had passed through the port in 1939, but, by 1941, the figure stood at just over 40,000 tons. However, the lend-lease agreement of that year led to a vast increase in the volume of supplies entering Britain from the United States, and, by 1942, 'the docks were almost working to full capacity again'. That year Southampton suffered only six attacks, with just one of these of the magnitude that the town had become accustomed to in its darkest days: a June morning saw the dropping of 72 bombs and 4,000 incendiaries.

However, the slowing of the attacks indeed convinced many that the worst of them were over. In April, the War Office began to assess the possibility of Southampton's role in a prospective large invasion of Europe, and in July a regional headquarters was established in rooms at the South Western Hotel. The following month thousands of British and Canadian troops passed through the town, taking part in an operation that would attempt to gain a foothold in France and measure the resolve of the occupying Germans there. However, the Dieppe Raid was a complete failure, with thousands killed, over 100 aircraft lost and none of the mission's objectives achieved. Lessons from the disaster had to be learnt before a full-scale invasion was attempted.

A year later, the American Army's 14th Major Port Transportation Corps came to the town, first establishing a base at the Maritime Chambers in the old docks and then relocating to the Civic Centre. Collaborating with the British Army and the Royal Navy, the railway company, council and even local retailers, the Corps began to plan the movement of American men and their supplies. Although for a time it appeared that the European invasion would take place that summer, another year passed before preparations were made and the time was right.

In 1943, there was just one air raid on Southampton and as time went on the town became more optimistic that the worst of its oppression was in the past. In mid-December a large crowd gathered at the Guildhall to hear a performance by the United States Army Choir, and there were particularly buoyant and hopeful scenes on New Year's Eve – a marked difference from the heart-warming but subdued atmosphere of three years earlier. This time the largest crowds since the outbreak of the war gathered to dance in the streets outside Holy Rood church and to sing songs. With the church bells still unusable, the bell-ringers instead turned to St Michael's, the bells of which were used, in the words of the *Daily Echo*, to 'ring in joyously the year of high hopes'. That night, in halls and hotels all over the town, thousands of Southampton's residents came together at celebratory dinner dances and looked to the future with genuine hope.

In the meantime, the plans for the Allied invasion of Europe – soon and forever known as D-Day – were finally nearing completion. 'The pressure on the accommodation at the docks was tremendous and raised gigantic problems,' recorded A. Temple Patterson, 'but they were overcome.' The scene at the quaysides was a hive of activity, with one of the most important tasks at hand being the construction of the Mulberry harbour that was to be towed across the Channel and used in the landing at Arromanches. To serve the great operation many new facilities were built, including rail links and warehousing, and enormous quantities of coal were stockpiled. Making the job even more challenging was the attempt, as far as possible, to camouflage the preparations in case enemy reconnaissance missions viewed the area from above. Also hidden from view, to a large extent, was the Avenue, transformed into an arterial tunnel by means of foliage camouflage suspended over the road. Thus protected from unwelcome eyes, thousands of men who would make up the invasion force made their way onto the Common to await their next orders: the town had become a huge camp, ammunition dump and airfield.

Great numbers of servicemen had been ferried to Britain on the Cunard liner *Queen Mary* and her sister ship *Queen Elizabeth*, which had entered service as a troopship in early 1940; she would not operate as a passenger liner until after the war. For many months, the two ships carried at least 10,000 men each on every voyage, leading Adolf Hitler to offer a sizeable bounty to any of his naval captains able to sink them. In Southampton docks the invasion of Europe drew ever closer, with ships so tightly packed that one observer speculated it might be possible to walk across them to the Isle of Wight. On 3 June, Winston Churchill came to view the preparations and the following day the loading of the armada was finished. After a delay because of bad weather, the D-Day plans were finally put into action on 5 June 1944, involving the transportation of over 160,000 troops in over 5,000 vessels in what King George VI called 'the greatest combined operation the world has ever seen'.

That evening Southampton and the rest of the nation held its collective breath, with even those in command unable to predict what the results would be. Of course, the enormous success of D-Day and its pivotal role in the outcome of the Second World War is well documented, but in many ways, it signalled the start of another period of intense work for the men and women of Southampton docks, as ongoing support was provided to the operation across the Channel. On one July day, seventy-five ships left for France and in the four months following D-Day, the port dealt with a level of military tonnage equal to that of the everyday trade seen in the whole of 1938. The vessels that returned to Southampton brought with them large numbers of prisoners of war, many of whom were accommodated in temporary pens in the town. Bernard Knowles observed that 'Southampton became a centre of marine operations on a scale that has no parallel in the world's history'; in 1944, over 22 million tons of shipping passed through the port. In October, the millionth American soldier to come through Southampton departed for France, and only three months later, the two millionth did likewise.

Soon the tide of war had swung decisively in favour of the Allies. At the start of May 1945, Berlin was breached and after five and a half years of torment, the end was finally in sight. It came a week later, although a universal sense of expectation preceded the official announcement by some hours. On 7 May, the feeling of anticipation was threatening to boil over into full-blown celebration. Flags and bunting flew all across the town, military vehicles raced back and forth, and in the words of one eyewitness, 'Old soldiers strutted the streets proudly wearing the ribbons they had won in the First World War'. At 12 a.m., a day of the greatest jubilation was heralded by the sirens, whistles and horns of the ships occupying the docks. As the joyous cacophony rang out, lights flashed across the sky and coloured rockets fizzed through the air. One witness reminisced:

> The most amazing thing I can recall from the whole period was when all the lights came back on again. We had all lived in darkness up to then due to the blackout and now, all of a sudden, there was this incredible light. It was just like fairyland and it was the real sign that the war was over.

By 12 p.m. on 8 May, the town centre was thronging with people awaiting the official broadcast from Winston Churchill; an estimated 20,000 gathered on the Civic Centre forecourt. Among them were representatives from all the armed forces (including American servicemen), as well as the police, fire service and the Home Guard. Corporation members, led by the mayor and sheriff, took their places on the entrance steps of the municipal offices as bells rang out across the town, flags waved and cheer after cheer of celebration went up from the crowds. At 3 p.m., the Civic Centre bells chimed and the throng fell silent to hear Churchill's words broadcast over a loudspeaker system. 'Hostilities will end officially', he declared, 'at one minute after midnight tonight ... The German war is therefore at an end.' At the conclusion of his speech great cheers resounded again, only to be quieted as 'O God Our Help In Ages Past' was played on the Guildhall organ and also relayed over the loudspeakers. The rector of St Mary's church, Canon Jolly, led a service of thanksgiving, after which the townspeople celebrated long into the evening.

Over the course of the war, Southampton had been attacked on almost sixty occasions, making it the seventh most bombed town or city in the country. Over 30,000 incendiaries were dropped on the town, as well as over 2,500 bombs and many more went uncounted as they landed in the Itchen, Test or Southampton Water; while 631 people lost their lives in the attacks and 1,800 were injured, half of them seriously. Nearly 1,000 buildings were demolished and over 40,000 were damaged, over 2,000 of them to the extent that they were beyond repair. Although many of the port's dry docks had been given over to preparations for D-Day for some considerable time, Harland & Wolff's repair yard alone had performed maintenance on over 7,000 vessels involved in the war effort.

Despite all their hardships, however, the townspeople began to look forward rather than back. That VE night, as Bernard Knowles recorded, 'the citizens of Southampton for the first time in five and a half years slept in peace … In the most terrible struggle of all time, they had remained faithful to their charge. They had fought the good fight.'

In the aftermath of the successful D-Day landings of June 1944, provision had to be made to transport essential supplies to the troops in northern France. Water, for example, was taken to the Continent in a convoy of oil tankers, which left from Southampton: in ten months over 100 million gallons were transported in this way. Equally if not more critical, however, was the ability to supply fuel across the Channel. The subject had first arisen as far back as April 1942, when a conversation between Geoffrey Lloyd (head of the Petroleum Warfare Department) and Lord Mountbatten produced a solution to the issue in the form of a pipeline. At first, it was thought that this proposal was unlikely to succeed, but Arthur Hartley, the chief engineer of the Anglo-Iranian Oil Company, hit on the idea of laying an enormous pipeline along the seabed. Prototypes were tested in a number of locations throughout 1942 and a full experiment took place in the Bristol Channel in December of that year. The following summer the project came to Southampton, when the Admiralty located part of the operation to a salvaged area of the bomb-damaged factory on the banks of the Itchen that had previously been involved in the manufacture of Spitfires. The building was restored to useful purpose when it became the hub of the endeavour, known as HMS Abatos. In the wake of D-Day the operation soon swung into action; the pipelines were shipped to Sandown on the Isle of Wight from where they were laid across the Channel to Cherbourg. At no point were the vessels taking part subjected to enemy attack. Once again, the project was a resounding success: vital supplies and means of communication were provided to the troops on the Continent, which helped to ensure that they were well positioned to continue the Allied war effort.

fifteen

CITY STATUS

With the coming of peace, Southampton turned its attention to the enormous task of repairing the damage caused by the Second World War. The most pressing job was the provision of housing. Of the town's 1939 population of around 180,000, approximately 60,000 had vacated the town at some point in the war, whether through service in the Armed Forces or evacuation. With their return, the lack of housing became more acute: the bombs had left many uninhabitable homes and a fragile infrastructure supporting the habitable ones. The temporary answer, at least, was the building of prefabricated houses, but plans for more ambitious housing estates were slower to reach fruition – to the annoyance of some sections of the community who were hearing of more efficient regeneration in other areas of the country.

Part of the problem stemmed from the Corporation's control of the rebuilding, which did not allow the contribution of private enterprise. The town centre, virtually flattened in many places, was even slower to recover because of the Council's compulsory purchase of much of the area, which provoked lengthy and controversial debate. Predictably prominent in the issue was Sidney Kimber, who had proposed the formation of a town restoration committee as far back as January 1941, in the immediate aftermath of the worst bombing raids. At the time, however, his idea was rejected, causing him to note with characteristic bravado, 'I feel certain the town has lost immeasurably by that adverse vote'.

In 1942, bold plans had been made, partially the work of Southampton's town planning officer. As the war was still continuing, the project was certainly optimistic and ambitious: obviously defeat was not a consideration. Included was a giant columnated shopping circus, a large recreation and exhibition area and a redeveloped pier incorporating a concert hall. Ultimately this plan and a number of others were abandoned, and it would not be until after the end

Southampton's post-war regeneration included the extension of the Rank Flour Mill, which had originally opened in 1934. (Courtesy of Associated British Ports)

of the war that the subject was properly tackled. By 1948, better progress was being made, but this was also the year in which Kimber suffered a second heart attack and he resigned from the Council that November. Struggling with deteriorating health, he published his memoirs in 1949 before his death in October of that year.

Railing against post-war Southampton's lack of diversified industry, Kimber commented that 'the town is now almost wholly dependent on its docks', and indeed significant priority was given to the resurgence of the passenger shipping trade. Certainly the return to passenger service of the *Queen Mary* and *Queen Elizabeth* was enormously important: the ships served as symbols of both the post-war restoration of normality and as reminders of the victorious war effort. In Churchill's words, 'The Queens challenged the fury of Hitlerism in the Battle of the Atlantic. Without their aid the day of final victory must unquestionably have been postponed.' In 1946 and 1947, the ships were refitted in Southampton, but the task was so vast that 1,500 workers were moved to the town from Glasgow's shipyards to assist. One of the giant quayside sheds in the docks was made into a temporary cafeteria to feed the swelling workforce.

Meanwhile, also under construction was the Ocean Terminal facility. Planning began a year after the end of the war, when an inspection party surveyed the ravaged docks and envisaged a new building 'with everything for the passenger under one roof, presented in the most favourable conditions'. With the return of the Cunard Queens, as well as the many other ships frequenting the port, the suitability of the passenger and cargo sheds were reassessed en masse. Having been built before the First World War, many of these sheds were now showing their inadequacies, especially in light of the increased sizes of the vessels they served. A number of them had suffered bomb damaged and there was an obvious chance to replace them with an improved facility. The new design provided a two-storey building on the quayside of the Ocean Dock – the upper floor for passengers and the lower dealing with luggage and cargo. The building was designed by C.B. Dromgoole in collaboration with the Fine Arts Commission and constructed by Staverton Builders of Totnes, Devon. Work was completed in 1950 and the Ocean Terminal was opened in July of that year by Prime Minister Clement Attlee. Appropriately enough the first ship to leave the new building after the opening ceremony was the *Queen Elizabeth*, and two days later the *Queen Mary* was the first to arrive there. A sleek, striking Art Deco design, the terminal was nearly 1,300ft long and incorporated a railway platform capable of housing two long trains together. The facilities provided for passengers on the upper floor were quite luxurious, certainly in the first class areas, offering an experience quite similar to that on board the liners themselves. On hand were shops, a bank, a writing room and travel agencies as well as telephones and telegraph facilities, and later even a room for use by the BBC. Telescopic gangways extended from the side of the building to join the doors of the ship in dock. How the inhabitants of Southampton's prefabricated cement bungalows felt when viewing this scene is open to speculation.

Of perhaps more pertinent interest to the town's public were the improvements in local public transport. Roads and bridges were modernised and, in 1950, trams were entirely replaced by buses, offering a far more widespread service particularly in the eastern side of the town. The following year, as part of the nationwide Festival of Britain project, the Bargate was renovated and the upper floor opened as a local history museum. Also in 1951, the area's economy benefited enormously from the completion of Esso's expansive oil refinery at Fawley on the western shore of Southampton Water. A refinery had first been

To accommodate the popular passenger liner trade, the Ocean Terminal was opened in 1950, and can be seen here with Cunard's *Queen Elizabeth* alongside it. After the trade had deteriorated, the Art Deco building was controversially demolished in 1983.

founded on the site in 1921 by the Atlantic Gulf and West Indies oil company, which was taken over by Esso. Work began in the autumn of 1949 and was finished just over two years later, with Prime Minister Clement Attlee returning to the area to perform the opening ceremony. The refinery made Southampton one of the main tanker ports of the country, and before long, the plant was receiving 150,000 barrels of crude oil every day.

The same year the census recorded a town population of just over 178,000, approaching the level seen before the Second World War. Three years later, there was another extension of the borough boundaries, increasing the population yet further. Incorporated on this occasion was the remaining area of Millbrook, stretching to Redbridge, while to the east Harefield and part of Thornhill were included. Meanwhile regeneration increased in pace, with permanent buildings replacing the makeshift structures erected in the aftermath of the war. By the mid-1950s Southampton was a regional shopping centre again, attracting a larger catchment area of customers than ever before. Testimony to this was the revitalisation of the Tyrrell & Green department store in Above Bar Street.

The shop had been founded by its eponymous owners in 1897 and sold to the John Lewis Partnership in the 1930s. Unsurprisingly its premises did not survive the Blitz unscathed, and temporary sites were used, first in Winchester and then back in Southampton, close to the Bargate. In 1954, the wreckage of the old shop was at last removed from the Above Bar Street site and work began on new buildings. The store reopened in May 1956 and its design found favour with Nikolaus Pevsner, who commented that 'few post war department stores, and no others in Southampton, have reached this standard'.

The majority of the retail area directly north of the Bargate, meanwhile, consisted of two-storey buildings in Portland stone, while Below Bar was initially only rebuilt as far south as Holy Rood church. The church itself was left as a ruin to commemorate the war's impact on the town and as a memorial to members of the Merchant Navy lost at sea; a plaque to that effect was unveiled there by the Bishop of Southampton in April 1957. In time, the area between Holy Rood and Town Quay became home to a number of warehouses involved in the fresh produce trade, with the gaps filled by offices. The High Street as a whole, so widely admired in days gone by, would never be the same again.

Above Bar Street also rose from the ashes of the Second World War and within fifteen years was a thriving retail area once more.

Above The Tyrrell & Green department store was a large landmark in Above Bar Street for many years. The store relocated to the West Quay shopping centre, and this building was demolished in 2010.

Right High Street at the turn of the century. (THP)

Like Holy Rood, St Mary's had been all but destroyed in the Blitz, but the town's oldest church was rebuilt. The first sections to be repaired were the tower and spire and the bells, which were recast from those damaged by bombs, were replaced and inaugurated at a special service held in June 1948. Work on the remainder of the restoration began in 1954, adhering broadly to the Victorian design of George Street, but with new enhancements and additions overseen by Romilly Craze. Pevsner, so enamoured with the Tyrrell & Green store, was less than impressed with the new St Mary's, and critical that a chance to construct something truly worthy of its status as the town's mother church had been wasted: 'What a failure to use artistic resources of a calibre to meet the challenge.' But when the work was completed in 1956, to the people of Southampton the rebuilding of St Mary's was more important symbolically than it ever could have been architecturally.

Further developments were also taking place in the new docks, themselves little over twenty years old, with the opening of another new passenger terminal. The building served the Union Castle vessels operating routes to South Africa and it was opened in January 1956 by G.P. Jooste, the High Commissioner for the Union of South Africa. While not quite as large or luxurious as Cunard's Ocean Terminal, the newer terminal offered much the same facilities, similarly divided over two floors. Notably, however, the building featured a sizeable and impressive mural by John Hutton, which related the story of Vasco da Gama's expedition around the Cape of Good Hope on his way to India in the seventeenth century.

To the west of the King George V Graving Dock a building project was soon under way that was the first of its kind in both Southampton and Great Britain. In February 1958, work began on what would become the country's first oilrig, built by Steel Structures Limited. The rig was completed later in the year and was launched in October with the name Orient Explorer. It was taken to Borneo to be used by the Shell Petroleum Company, leaving the docks in February 1959. At the same time a new form of sea transport was also being developed. Southampton was the focal point of the evolution of Christopher Cockerell's hovercraft design, a concept taken up by the National Development Corporation in 1958. Local seafaring expertise was brought to bear on the project, and, in 1959, a prototype craft made its first journey on Southampton Water. A passenger service to the Isle of Wight began in 1962 to complement the continued services of the Red Funnel ferries.

Such new amenities served an ever increasing town population: the census of 1961 showed that for the first time Southampton was home to more than 200,000 residents. In 1958, Mayor Hammond had petitioned the queen, requesting that the town be given city status, and although it did not come to pass at the time, progress in the next few years saw this granted in February 1964. The event was not marked by a grand civic occasion, but there was a brief ceremony held in the mayor's parlour. Mayor Pugh read a letter from the Home Office, which revealed that 'Her Majesty the Queen has been graciously pleased to raise the town and county of the town of Southampton to the title and dignity of a city.' Thus, an ambition expressed by Sidney Kimber when he became mayor in November 1918 was realised fifteen years after his death.

The style of the post-war rebuilding of St Mary's may not have pleased architectural historian Nikolaus Pevsner, but to this day, it remains the 'mother church' of the city.

One of the factors that helped Southampton to become a city was the growth of the university. In 1952, this institution had been granted a royal charter, meaning that it could award its own degrees, and although there was a brief decline in student numbers around this time, they had risen steadily since. As the increase was forecast to continue an entire new complex of buildings was proposed, and Basil Spence was commissioned to prepare plans in 1956, the same year that work began on his design for the rebuilding of Coventry Cathedral. One of the most prominent elements in the plan was a new theatre, to be incorporated into the proposed Faculty of Arts following a donation from the Nuffield Foundation in 1960. Construction of this part of the project started in 1961, and the Nuffield Theatre was formally opened by the veteran stage actress, Sybil Thorndike, in March 1964.

Ocean-going developments continued as well. Also in 1964, an additional car ferry route connected Southampton to Cherbourg, the first service to depart from the town using the new 'drive-on, drive-off' vessels. The inaugural sailing took place in May 1964 when the Thoresen ferry, *Viking*, left the Outer Dock for France. The service to Le Havre also prospered, and within three years, more freight traffic left for that port from Southampton than from Dover. The Outer Dock was beginning to show its age, however, and, in 1965, approval was given to build two new terminals to serve the Continental ferries, which in 1967 began operating a route to Bilbao. Nevertheless, the Outer Dock was reno-

The ancient Bargate still dominates the city centre.

The old Outer Dock was converted in the 1960s to become home to a number of European ferry services. It was officially renamed the Princess Alexandra Dock in 1967. (Courtesy of Associated British Ports)

vated and rechristened the Princess Alexandra Dock in a ceremony to mark its completion in July 1967. Alongside it was a passenger ferry terminal, 167ft in length, with a viewing area from which travellers could observe the vessels coming and going. The updated facility was soon used by Jersey Lines Limited, thus briefly returning a Channel Islands service to Southampton following its earlier transfer to Weymouth in 1962.

The traditional North Atlantic passenger routes had for some years suffered because of competition from air travel, and their time was soon to come to an end. Symptomatic was the decline of the Terminus station, where tradition- ally passengers had alighted before their onward journeys overseas. The small connecting line to Town Quay had been removed in 1952 and the station was omitted from updates to the Waterloo–Bournemouth line in 1965. Terminus operated its last passenger services in the autumn of 1966 and its mail offices closed the following year. *Queen Mary* undertook a farewell cruise in 1967 before returning to Southampton, and shortly afterwards leaving again in a departure laden with equal parts of pageantry and emotion. Her ultimate destination was Long Beach in California, where she remains as a hotel, con- ference centre and museum. A year later, *Queen Elizabeth* also left for the last time, although her dawn sailing time did not allow the same sense of occasion bestowed upon her older sister. She was converted into the Seawise University and moored in Hong Kong Harbour; in January 1972, she tragically caught fire and sank.

Cunard replaced the two legends of the Atlantic with *Queen Elizabeth 2*, built on the same Clyde slipway as her illustrious predecessors. To make the new ship more commercially viable she was designed to be able to operate both on cruises and the transatlantic route. Her maiden voyage to New York began in May 1969, departing from the specifically built Queen Elizabeth II Terminal, opened by the monarch herself in July 1966. By October 1969, P&O had moved all its passenger operations to Southampton, including the Australasian routes on which its two premier liners, *Oriana* and *Canberra*, would work for some years, until they too joined the cruising side of the industry.

Elsewhere in the docks, meanwhile, other progress was being made. The volume of containerised cargoes had been growing rapidly in the 1960s and the benefits of this form of transport were revealed in a 1967 investigation by the British Transport Docks Board. The economies of scale affected would, it was predicted, lead to a dramatic reduction in shipping costs, and Southampton's status as a location capable of handling the largest vessels in the world made it the obvious choice for the construction of a new container port. Prophetically, the British Transport Docks Board already owned 200 acres of

Southampton's former Terminus railway station, now converted into a casino.

In the same year that the first Boat Show took place, Southampton also welcomed the new Cunarder *Queen Elizabeth 2*, a modern replacement for her departed predecessors *Queen Elizabeth* and *Queen Mary*. She operated from the port until 2008, by which time she had become the longest-serving Cunard vessel. (Courtesy of Associated British Ports)

land to the west of the previous docks expansion of the 1930s. The Board had bought the site after the Second World War and approval was now received from the government to develop a container port there. Work began in 1967 and two huge berths were completed in a little over eighteen months, by which time the two largest cranes in the country were in position there. No grand ceremonial opening was performed, but, in October 1968, a civic reception formally welcomed the cargo ship, *Teniers*, to the quayside. Business expanded so rapidly that within five years a further three berths were added.

Shipping was not the only industry going through a period of change at this time. The Ordnance Survey cartography offices had first come to the town in the early 1840s when, after fifty years of being housed in the Tower of London, a fire destroyed the department in November 1841 and new accommodation was sought. With seemingly arbitrary reasoning, the location chosen was Southampton – specifically the old military barracks at the southern end of the Avenue, which at the time served as a home for orphans. Over the ensuing century, the Ordnance Survey made huge advances in cartography techniques, and in the First World War, the Southampton offices supplied the army with a staggering 32 million maps. The Second World War was equally noteworthy to the establishment, but for entirely different reasons. The Blitz of 30 November 1940 severely damaged the London Road buildings, preventing meaningful operation on the site and many valuable and irreplaceable maps were lost forever. Some staff were relocated within Southampton, while others moved to newly provided offices in Surrey in 1942 and 1943. As circumstances returned to normal after the war and as advances in the industry continued, it soon became clear that entirely new offices would have to be constructed. Plans were made for an enormous new building in Maybush capable of housing several thousand staff and it was opened by Queen Elizabeth II in May 1969.

Later that year an event began that has taken place annually ever since – the Southampton Boat Show. This was designed to complement the London event held at Earl's Court, with the added advantage that boats could actually be viewed in the water. Invariably the centre of the show is at Mayflower Park, a recreation area to the west of the pier that was created at the same time as the docks extension of the 1930s. By the early 1970s, over 50,000 visitors a year were attending the Boat Show and in recent years, that figure has comfortably exceeded 100,000, with over 600 exhibitors displaying their wares.

In the late 1960s, the docks were extended again to include the container port, which has thrived to this day. (Courtesy of Associated British Ports)

The Southampton Boat Show, seen here in the mid-1970s, began in 1969 and has since become an annual international attraction. (Courtesy of Associated British Ports)

For those with an interest in sport and leisure, but perhaps with more humble means than the average customer at the Boat Show, the inordinately hot summer of 1976 brought a weekend that will live long in the memories of all supporters of Southampton Football Club. The club had been formed in 1885 as the St Mary's Young Men's Association, playing for the first few years either on the Common or at the town's cricket grounds in Northlands Road and St Mary's Road. After joining the Southern League in 1894 the club moved to a new purpose-built stadium four years later: the Dell was located in the Polygon area of the town and was the team's home for more than a century. By now known simply as Southampton Football Club, the team reached the final of the Football Association Cup in both 1900 and 1902, but it would be over seventy years before victory in the competition was finally achieved.

In May 1976, the team travelled to Wembley Stadium in London to take on Manchester United in the FA Cup Final. Southampton, being in the second division of English football, was considered the underdog, and many saw the match as a foregone conclusion. Against all odds, however, the team more than equalled their opponents and a goal from Bobby Stokes late in the second half won the game and the cup, sending half of the great stadium into delirium. The following day, the players and coaching staff returned to the city to tour the streets and parade the trophy, amid scenes reminiscent of those witnessed on

VE Day over thirty years earlier; some estimates have put the crowd numbers in the region of 200,000. Nick Holmes, who was born in Southampton and spent his entire playing career with the club, recalled, 'I think we were all shocked by the reception we got. The trip around town was expected to take half an hour, but it lasted half the day.' His teammate Mel Blyth also remembered, 'I have never seen so many people or so many tough, six foot men, kneeling and weeping in the street.'

The following year a permanent bridge was finally completed to connect the Chapel area of the city with Woolston, and in doing so, the floating bridge that had operated since 1836 was replaced. Plans for such a bridge had first been put forward in the 1930s, but it was not until 1974 that a design was finalised and a building contract awarded. After three years of construction, the bridge was completed in May 1977. Its position closely resembled the route taken by the old floating bridge and the central span of the reinforced concrete structure measured some 350ft. The first member of the public to cross it was Edith Park of Sholing, who dramatically declared herself 'thrilled to death' at the privilege. At the start of June, the mayor conducted a more formal inaugural journey across the bridge, and a yet more formal opening ceremony was conducted by Princess Alexandra the following month.

In the meantime, the floating bridge had made its final crossing at 10 p.m. on 11 June. It was an emotional occasion viewed by some 5,000 spectators, who congregated on the shores of the Itchen and indeed on the new bridge itself: 'Every vantage point was claimed. On roofs and parapets, walls and pavements, cars and buses.' While the benefits of the new bridge were undeniable, over the years the floating bridge had engendered a great deal of affection; it had also been immortalised in a painting by L.S. Lowry and a folksong by Southampton songwriter Mike Sadler. This song was recorded and released to mark the demise of the chain bridge and proved popular locally. In almost a century and a half of operation, thirteen barges had plied their trade back and forth across the Itchen; one of these was preserved and became an entertainment venue on the River Hamble. Many who experienced a journey on the floating bridge will contend that it had a magical character all of its own.

Unexpectedly, almost thirty-seven years after VE Day, in the spring of 1982, Southampton once more found itself embroiled in a military conflict. Escalating political tensions with Argentina resulted in the Falklands War, with the sovereignty of the small islands in the South Atlantic at the centre of the dispute. War broke out at the beginning of April, and Southampton was soon

Southampton once again found itself embroiled in conflict with the advent of the Falklands War in 1982. P&O's liner *Canberra*, a regular visitor to the port in peacetime, made an emotional return up Southampton Water at the end of the hostilities.

heavily involved in the operation, not least because its two most famous passenger liners were called into action. Within a few days, P&O's *Canberra* was back in the port and after an intensive forty-eight-hour conversion (including the installation of a helicopter landing pad) she departed for the Falklands on 9 April. In May *Queen Elizabeth 2* was also requisitioned and similarly refitted, and took 3,000 troops to the south Atlantic. She returned to Southampton a month later to be met by Queen Elizabeth the Queen Mother aboard the royal yacht *Britannia*. Three days after the return of the *Queen Elizabeth 2* the Argentines surrendered, marking the end of a war that had lasted only seventy-four days but had taken over 900 lives on both sides in total. The following month, after sailing over 25,000 miles, *Canberra* also arrived safely back in England, accompanied up Southampton Water by a huge flotilla of vessels of all sizes. She docked at the quayside amid emotional scenes, with families and friends celebrating the homecoming of their loved ones. Once again, in Britain's time of need, Southampton had proved itself equal to the task.

In recent years, Southampton has continued to grow, albeit at a steady but unspectacular rate, and now has a population estimated at over 230,000 people. The mainstay of the city, naturally, is still its maritime industry, although the passenger trade has undergone its own changes: the docks may at first glance appear to have altered little in the last thirty years, but many features have been lost. A year after the Falklands War the Ocean Terminal was demolished, which at the time seemed to signal the breaking of the last link with the era of the *Queen Mary* and *Queen Elizabeth*. There appeared to be little hope that the glamorous days of ocean travel would ever come back to Southampton, even though the port's two most recognisable sights, *Queen Elizabeth 2* and *Canberra*, continued to operate regular services.

The importance of the city's coastal location and its unbreakable link with the water continued to be reflected in its progress, however. Ongoing expansion of the university led to the construction of the Southampton Oceanography Centre (later its name was changed to the National Oceanography Centre), situated alongside the Empress Dock. The facility was opened by the Duke of Edinburgh in 1996 and specialises in various kinds of marine research and technology undertaken by over 1,000 staff and students. The centre is also the base from which a number of state-of-the-art research vessels operate, both locally and much further afield.

Increasingly, other new developments in the city related to leisure pastimes and retail. In the mid-1990s, the Leisure World complex was built on West Quay Road, housing a multi-screen cinema, casino, nightclubs, bars and restaurants. Predictably but sadly this sounded the final death knell for cinemas throughout the city centre and the suburbs, although many had already closed to be either demolished or altered for other uses. Soon afterwards, only a few hundred yards away, work began on the West Quay Shopping Centre, which was largely built on the site of the old Pirelli factory on Western Esplanade. West Quay opened in the autumn of 2000 and is regarded as one of the premier shopping malls in the country, accommodating stores of all manner and size. One of these is the John Lewis department store, which relocated from its Above Bar Street home after nearly seventy years of trading, changing its name from Tyrrell & Green in the process.

The opening of the West Quay Shopping Centre seemed to reflect a growth in affluence and prosperity, and to complement it the start of the twenty-first century saw a significant upturn in the cruising industry, even including the

The old and the new collide as the ancient town defences overlook West Quay Shopping
Centre, 2011.

Cunard's liner *Queen Victoria* in Southampton docks, 2011.

reintroduction of a transatlantic route from Southampton. Spearheading the new era was Queen Mary 2, which entered service in 2004 and replaced *Queen Elizabeth 2* as Cunard's flagship. The following year, *Queen Elizabeth 2* became the longest serving vessel in Cunard's history, but as is so often the case the start of one era signalled the end of another, and, in 2007, it was announced that the ship would be sold and become a floating hotel in Dubai. There was still time, however, for a remarkable final eighteen months of her seagoing career. In April 2008, *Queen Elizabeth 2* joined *Queen Mary 2* and another new Cunarder, *Queen Victoria*, in Southampton – the first time three Cunard Queens had been present in the port together. That autumn *Queen Elizabeth 2* and *Queen Mary 2* made a historic tandem crossing to New York, returning to Southampton in October. The ship left the docks for the last time the following month, despite appeals from some quarters that she should either remain in service or be permanently berthed in her homeport. With the departure of *Queen Elizabeth 2* (and the earlier retirement of *Canberra* in 1997) the old guard had gone forever, but a new group of ships has now taken up the mantle and there appears to be no shortage of customers who wish to experience trips of a lifetime aboard them. Another passenger terminal was opened in 2009 and the largest vessels in the world are frequent visitors to the port. As long as the Itchen and the Test continue to flow into the Solent, Southampton's future is assured.

SOUTHAMPTON SPEEDWAY

As Southampton continued its post-war recovery the entertainment of its citizens also began to return to a condition closer to that seen in 1939. Speedway in the town had begun in 1928 at the Banister Court Stadium, adjacent to Hampshire's County Cricket Ground. The venue was built on a site that had previously been home to a school and a lake was filled in to enable its development; the original intention was to provide a home for greyhound racing in Southampton, and indeed this was the first event held at the stadium in August 1928. However, it soon became clear that attendances were too small to be economically viable, and, inspired by recent 'dirt-track racing' in London, it was suggested that the same spectacle be held in Southampton. Only a few weeks later the inaugural meeting went ahead, and future meetings were watched by enthusiastic crowds on Wednesdays and Saturdays, thrilled to see the well-known riders of the day taking to the track. The following year a league was formed. Although attendances were initially very good, they fluctuated a great deal over the ensuing years, and thus so did the fortunes of the stadium. The 1930s ended with the Southampton Saints (as they were known) reaching the top tier of the national league, but although some meetings were held in 1940 competition was postponed until after the war. Speedway resumed in 1947, and despite some further instability, in the sport as a whole as well as the team, something of a golden era dawned for the Saints. The team performed well in the late 1950s and achieved great success in cup competitions in 1961, but the following year the national league title was at last secured. This pinnacle was followed by a swift decline, however: the year 1963 brought problems with team personnel and the final blow came when it was decided to sell the Banister Court Stadium for redevelopment. The last meeting was held in October 1963, after which the roar of speedway in Southampton was silenced forever.

BIBLIOGRAPHY

Adams, B. ed., *The Missing Link: The Story of the Itchen Bridge* (Southampton: Southampton City Council, 1977).

Addison, W., *English Spas* (London: Batsford, 1951).

Anonymous, *Historic Buildings of Southampton* (Southampton: Southampton Museums Publications, 1963).

Arnott, A., *Maritime Southampton* (Derby: Breedon Books, 2002).

Arnott, A., *Southampton: Gateway to the World* (Stroud: The History Press, 2010).

Baker, S., *Ancient Rome* (BBC Books, 2006).

Barker, J., *Agincourt: The King, The Campaign, The Battle* (London: Abacus, 2005).

Bissell, A., *Southampton's Children of the Blitz* (Trowbridge: Red Post Books, 2001).

Blair, P.H., *An Introduction to Anglo-Saxon England* (London: Cambridge University Press, 1956).

Boyle, A., *Trenchard: Man of Vision* (London: Collins, 1962).

Brown, J., *The Illustrated History of Southampton's Suburbs* (Derby: Breedon Books, 2004).

Cam, H., *England Before Elizabeth* (London: Hutchinson, 1950).

Carpenter Turner, B., *A History of Hampshire* (Chichester: Phillimore, 1978).

Coles, R.J., *Southampton's Historic Buildings* (Southampton: City of Southampton Society, 1981).

Colquhoun, K., *A Thing In Disguise: The Visionary Life of Joseph Paxton* (London: Harper Perennial, 2004).

Cotton, M.A. and Gathercole, P.W., *Excavations at Clausentum, Southampton 1951–1954* (London: HMSO, 1958).

Davies, Revd J.S, *A History of Southampton* (Exeter: Hampshire Books, 1989).

Douch, R. ed., *Visitors' Descriptions of Southampton: 1540–1956* (Southampton, City of Southampton, 1978).

Englefield, H.C. and J. Bullar, *A Walk Through Southampton: Including A Survey of Its Antiquities* (1841).

Eustace, P., *Southampton Speedway* (Stroud: Tempus Publishing, 2002).

Frankland, C., D. Hyslop and S. Jemima, *Southampton Blitz: The Unofficial Story* (Southampton: Southampton City Council, 1990).

Gardiner, J., *The Blitz: The British Under Attack* (London: Harper Collins, 2010).

Gardiner, R., *The History of the White Star Line* (Hersham: Ian Allen, 2001).

Gallaher, T., *A Century of Southampton* (Stroud: Sutton Publishing, 2000).

Granville, A.B., *Spas of England Volume 2: The Midlands and South* (Bath: Adams and Dart, 1971).

Harvey, J., *English Medieval Architects: A Biographical Dictionary* (Gloucester: Alan Sutton Publishing, 1984).

Hattersley, R., *The Edwardians* (London: Abacus, 2006).

Hoare, P., *Spike Island: The Memory of a Military Hospital* (London: Fourth Estate, 2001).

Hodgson, J., *Southampton Castle* (Horndean: Milestone Publications/Southampton City Council).

Holdsworth, P., *Excavations at Melbourne Street, Southampton 1971–1976* (London: Council for British Archaeology, 1980).

Hunter-Blair, P., *An Introduction to Anglo-Saxon England* (London: Cambridge University Press, 1956).

Hyslop, D., A. Forsyth and S. Jemima, *Titanic Voices: Memories from the Fateful Voyage* (Stroud: Sutton Publishing/Southampton City Council, 1997).

James, L., *The Rise and Fall of the British Empire* (London: Abacus, 1995).

Kalush, W., and L. Sloman, *The Secret Life of Houdini: The Making of the World's Greatest Mystifier* (London: Simon & Schuster, 2007).

Kemp, A., *Southampton At War 1939–45* (Southampton: Ensign Publications, 1989).

Kilby, P., *Southampton Through the Ages* (Southampton: Computational Mechanics Publications, 1997).

Kimber, S., *Thirty Eight Years of Public Life in Southampton* (Southampton: privately published, 1949).

Knowles, B., *Southampton: The English Gateway* (London: Hutchinson, 1951).

Leonard, A.G.K., *Stories of Southampton Streets* (Southampton: Paul Cave, 1984).

Leonard, A.G.K., *More Stories of Southampton Streets* (Southampton: Paul Cave, 1989).

Lockyer, R., *Tudor and Stuart Britain 1471–1714* (Harlow: Longman, 1985).

Longford, E., *Victoria R I* (London: Pan, 1966).

Loyn, H.R., *Anglo-Saxon England and the Norman Conquest* (Harlow: Longman, 1962).

McCutcheon, C., *Port of Southampton* (Stroud: Tempus Publishing, 2005).

Manns, T. and Bull, D., *Tie A Yellow Ribbon: How Saints Won The Cup* (Bristol: Hagiology Publishing, 2006).

Maxtone-Graham, J., *Cunard: 150 Glorious Years* (Newton Abbot: David & Charles, 1989).

Mitchell, G., *R.J. Mitchell: Schooldays to Spitfire* (Stroud: The History Press, 2009).

Monkhouse, F.J. ed., *A Survey of Southampton and Its Region* (Southampton: Southampton University Press, 1964).

Morgan, J.B. and P. Peberdy, eds, *Collected Essays on Southampton*, (Southampton: Southampton City Council, 1968).

Mortimer, I., *1415: Henry V's Year of Glory* (Bodley Head, London, 2009).

Neillands, R., *The Hundred Years War* (Routledge, London, 1990).

Oxley, J. ed., *Excavations at Southampton Castle* (Stroud: Southampton City Museums/Alan Sutton Publishing, 1986).

Pannell, J.P.M., *Old Southampton Shores* (Newton Abbot: David & Charles, 1967).

Patterson, A.T., *The University of Southampton* (Southampton: University of Southampton, 1962).

Patterson, A.T., *A Selection From The Southampton Corporation Journals 1815–35 and Borough Council Minutes 1835–47* (Southampton: University of Southampton, 1965).

Patterson, A.T., *Southampton: A Biography* (London: Macmillan, 1970).

Peckham, I., *Southampton and D-Day* (Southampton: Southampton City Council, 1994).

Pevsner, N., and D. Lloyd, *Buildings of England: Hampshire and the Isle of Wight* (London: Penguin, 1967).

Philbrick, N., *Mayflower: A Story of Courage, Community and War* (London: Viking, 2006).

Platt, C., *Medieval Southampton: The Port and Trading Community AD 1000–1600* (London: Routledge & Kegan Paul, 1973).

Porter, S., *The Great Plague* (Stroud: Sutton Publishing, 1999).

Pryor, F., *Britain In The Middle Ages* (London: Harper Perennial, 2007).

Rance, A., *Shipbuilding in Victorian Southampton* (Southampton: Southampton University Industrial Archaeology Group, 1981).

Rance, A., *Southampton: An Illustrated History* (Portsmouth: Milestone Publications/City of Southampton, 1986).

Reynolds, D., *Task Force: The Illustrated History of the Falklands War* (Stroud: Sutton Publishing, 2002).

Richards, J.D., *Viking Age England* (Stroud: Tempus Publishing, 2000).

Roberts, E., *Hampshire Houses 1250–1700: Their Dating and Development* (Winchester: Hampshire County Council, 2003).

Russell, C.F., *A History of King Edward VI School Southampton* (Cambridge: privately published, 1940).

Roussel, M., *The Story of Southampton Docks* (Derby, Breedon Books, 2009).

Sandell, E.M., *Southampton Cavalcade* (Southampton: G.F. Wilson & Co., 1953).

Schama, S., *A History of Britain Volume 1: 3000 BC–AD 1603 At The Edge Of The World?* (London: BBC Books, 2000).

Schama, S., *A History of Britain Volume 2: 1603–1776 The British Wars* (London: BBC Books, 2001).

Schama, S., *A History of Britain Volume 3: 1776–2000 The Fate of Empire* (London: BBC Books, 2002).

Strong, R., *The Story of Britain* (London: Hutchinson, 1996).

Sumption, J., *Trial By Battle: The Hundred Years War Volume 1* (London: Faber and Faber, 1990).

Taylor, A.J.P., *The Origins of the Second World War* (London: Penguin, 1964).

Webster, N.W., *Joseph Locke: Railway Revolutionary* (London: George Allen & Unwin, 1970).

White, B., S. Jemima and D. Hyslop, *Dream Palaces: Going to the Pictures in Southampton* (Southampton: Southampton City Council, 1996).

Williams, R.A., *The London and South Western Railway Volume One: The Formative Years* (Newton Abbot: David & Charles, 1968).

Wilson, A.N., *The Victorians* (London: Hutchinson, 2002).

Wilson, A.N., *After The Victorians* (London: Hutchinson, 2005).

Wolmar, C., *Fire and Steam: How the Railways Transformed Britain* (London: Atlantic, 2007).

INDEX

If you enjoyed this book, you may also be interested in ...

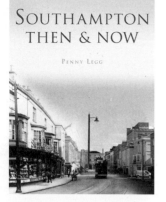

Southampton Then & Now
PENNY LEGG

The major port city of Southampton has a rich heritage, which is uniquely reflected in this fascinating new compilation. Contrasting a rare selection of archive images with full-colour modern photographs, this book reveals the ever-changing faces and buildings of Southampton. Covering local landmarks, pubs and hotels, churches, parks, transport, work and leisure, this is a wide-ranging look at the city's colourful history. This volume will appeal to all who know and love the city.

978 0 7524 5693 5

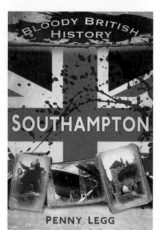

Bloody British History: Southampton
PENNY LEGG

The people of Southampton have had a lot to put up with over the centuries. If the Danes or the French weren't attacking it, pirates from further along were. Treasonous plots were hatched behind its ancient walls and mutiny hit its shipping. This book looks at such bloody events as the Black Death in the city, what happens when you cross a king, the ill-fated *Titanic* and the Blitz. Yes, the best bits of Southampton's history are surely the bloodiest!

978 0 7524 7110 5

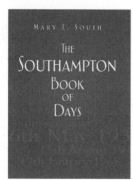

The Southampton Book of Days
MARY L. SOUTH

Taking you through the year day by day, *The Southampton Book of Days* contains quirky, eccentric, shocking, amusing and important events and facts from different periods in the history of the city. Featuring hundreds of snippets of information gleaned from the vaults of Southampton's archives and covering the social, criminal, political, religious, agricultural, industrial and military history of the region, it will delight residents and visitors alike.

978 0 7524 6534 0